BIG BEND

BIG

by
J. O. LANGFORD
with
FRED GIPSON

Photographs by
HENRY B. DU PONT
and
JOE W. LANGFORD

Drawings by
HAL STORY

BEND

A Homesteader's Story

UNIVERSITY OF TEXAS PRESS, AUSTIN

International Standard Book Number 978-0-292-70734-4
Library of Congress Catalog Card Number 73-91002

Second Edition
Tenth paperback printing, 2009

∞The paper used in this book meets the minimum
requirements of ANSI/NISO Z39.48-1992 (R1997)
(Permanence of Paper).

To

HENRY B. DU PONT

who knows and loves the Big Bend

PUBLISHER'S NOTE

This new edition of *Big Bend* is identical in text with the first edition published in 1952. Substitutions have been made for some of the photographs and others added.

Henry B. "Hank" du Pont of Wilmington, Delaware, was responsible for the existence of this book in the first place. During one of his trips to the Big Bend, a country which fascinated him, he met J. O. Langford and encouraged him to write his story. He also made it possible for Fred Gipson, author of *Hound Dog Man*, *Old Yeller*, and many other books, to collaborate with Mr. Langford in producing the final manuscript. Most of the splendid photographs which illustrate this work were also made by Mr. du Pont, others by Mr. Langford's son Joe. We are grateful to Mrs. Henry B. du Pont of Wilmington and to Mrs. Lovie M. Whitaker of Alpine for making these pictures available.

J. O. Langford, Fred Gipson, and Henry B. du Pont, all have died since this book was first published. In a very real sense this new edition is a memorial to them.

University of Texas Press

Illustrations

BIG BEND

One

OURS MUST HAVE SEEMED a strange procession as we headed south out of Alpine, Texas, that May morning. Even in 1909, when animal-drawn vehicles were the customary mode of travel, I could see curiosity in the eyes of early risers who watched us leave town.

Out in front, astride a belled gray mare, rode the lanky Mexican boy, Enrique Díaz. Behind him and following the mare, plodded eight Mexican burros, drawing an ore wagon piled high with our household goods and all the provisions I could afford to buy. On top of all this rode the squat and cheerful Juan Salas.

Chained to the ore wagon came our buckboard, with my wife Bessie and me sitting on the springseat, our eighteen-months-old daughter Lovie between us. Tex, our female collie dog, brought up the rear, padding along in the hoof-trampled dust, now and then leaving the wagon trace to sniff inquisitively at a gopher hole.

Stretching away from us on all sides were great sweeps of prairie, lushly green with tall grasses, splotched with yellow and blue and red patches of wild flowers; studded here and there with up-thrusting, creamy white blooms of flowering sotol. Cattle grazed on the prairie, and horses; and we were hardly out of town before we disturbed a band of antelope, who flared their short tails like white fans and bounded away at unbelievable speed.

To the south and west, lifting itself above the rolling foothills, rose the ragged crest of a mountain range, its sharp peaks a misty blue in the distance.

Somewhere beyond that range, and beyond the Chisos Mountains on the other side, one hundred and fifteen miles away, lay our destination. There, in the country where the Rio Grande made its big bend, lay a three-section homestead for us. It was a homestead we'd never seen. A homestead on which I'd gambled almost everything I had, without even looking the place over first.

This was a fantastic country, like none I'd ever seen, like no other I've seen since. And, looking back on it now, I can see that ours was a fantastic situation. A chronically ill man of thirty-one, a travelling salesman out of Mississippi, using up his last few dollars to take his wife and baby to a homestead in the wild, unknown country of the Texas Big Bend.

On the face of it, such a gamble was sheer madness. The odds were all against us. Homesteading anywhere is for the strong and vigorous man, not for one whose health is broken by years of malaria and indigestion. Then there was Bessie. A city girl, pregnant now, and with no money to bring her back to civilization when her time came. And Lovie, still a baby, and so far from a doctor.

We still had a little over two hundred dollars in the bank at Midland, but I knew it would squeeze that money to feed us for the next three years of continuous occupancy that the homestead law required.

And that wasn't taking into account the three hundred dollars more we were required to spend in improvements in those three years. That three hundred I'd have to earn yet, in some manner I couldn't foresee. And then, after that, there'd still be the annual payments on the land to meet.

[4]

One serious accident, and we'd go under. Or maybe even without an accident—if I couldn't figure out some way to provide for us and earn some cash over and above our living. What if my health grew worse, so that I became a helpless invalid? What would become of Bessie and the babies out here in this lonely wilderness if I should die?

By conscious effort, I steered my mind away from such dismal thoughts. I made myself think of what we had in our favor. To begin with, there were Bessie and I, and our faith in each other. Bessie knew as well as I what we were up against; but she was willing to go anywhere in the world that there was a faint hope of restoring my health.

And our hope lay now in the hot spring on our new property. The spring that boiled up out of a rock ledge on the river bank and spilled its medicinal waters into the Rio Grande.

This search for my health had started years ago when I'd contracted malaria in my home state of Mississippi. I'd been just a big kid then, and I'd forget I had malaria the minute I recovered from one bout with it and wouldn't think about it till the next attack.

But too many bouts weakened me badly and left me with such a torn-up stomach that I could hardly eat. I began listening to the people who said "Go West, young man!"

On the day I finally made up my mind to leave the dank swamp country of Mississippi, I was out in the middle of my father's cotton field, picking cotton. And right then, without mulling the subject over any more, I dropped my cotton sack and walked away. I went to my room and put on my seersucker suit. I packed my ten-dollar blue serge, a couple of shirts, two celluloid collars, and three pairs of socks. I was getting away from this fever-ridden country of calomel, chill tonic, and quinine. That day I bought a ticket for as far west as my last five dollars would take me.

But in less than two years, I was back again, too ill with malaria to take care of myself. I spent several months at home in bed where my mother could look after me. It was a long time before I was finally able to go to work again.

This time I took a job as a travelling salesman for a firm in Nashville, Tennessee. I worked a territory covering Louisiana and Alabama. And it was at this time that I met Bessie.

I was singing in the choir at a little church in Tupelo, Mississippi, and I can remember still how she looked when she came in. She was a big girl, with heavy blonde hair looped and piled high on her head. She was late and flustered, so that her face glowed a pretty pink.

I stopped singing, leaving the choir short one bass. I gulped, watching the girl walk to her seat. "That's the one for me," I thought. "That's the girl."

I lost no time getting acquainted, and soon began such an urgent courtship that I crowded Bessie into marrying me. It was the smartest thing I ever did.

For awhile, Bessie and I lived in Montgomery, Alabama, and she occasionally went with me on my selling trips out in the territory. But my health continued to be bad, and as soon as I thought I'd saved enough money to quit my job, we moved to Dallas.

In Dallas, I was some better; but I was still a long way from being well. Before long, we decided to make another move. We went farther west, to Midland, Texas.

And still I was a sick man. I was able to work only part of the time and was having to spend too large a portion of my income on doctor bills and medicine.

So once again, I had decided to try to move farther west, still in the hope that I could regain my health. By this time, Lovie had been born; she was eighteen months old now. I had left Bessie and Lovie in Midland while I went to Alpine to look around. I was hoping to hear of some school land for homesteading.

I registered at the Alpine Hotel, and it was in the lobby that same morning that I heard a man tell of the hot mineral springs down in the Big Bend country.

"They'll cure anything!" he vowed. "Stomach trouble, rheumatism, all sorts of skin diseases."

A less desperate man than I might have discounted such a sweeping statement. But any man in my wretched physical condition would have listened.

I moved closer to the man, trying to catch every word he said. "There's no mistake about it," he went on. "Plenty of sick folks have gone down there and drunk that water and bathed in it and come back well. The Indians were using it long before white men ever got out this way. They chipped themselves out a bathtub, right in solid rock, where they could bathe all they liked."

I introduced myself to the man and told him my trouble. I asked him if he thought the springs would help me. He told me he was sure they would.

"I wonder why it is," I asked, "that I've never heard of those springs before. It looks like somebody would have tried to develop them like they've done at Hot Springs, Arkansas."

"Oh, nobody could go down there and live long enough for that," the man answered.

"Why not?" I asked.

"Nothing down there but rattlesnakes and bandit Mexicans," he said. "And it's too far away from anywhere for a sick man to feel like going there to get cured. That damned country promises more and gives less than any place I ever saw." Then he grinned. "The Mexicans say that when God was making the world, he used up the best of the material before he got to the Big Bend country and just dumped the leavings down there. There's nothing down there that don't have claws or thorns or a sting to it."

"Is there anyone on the spring now?" I asked.

The man shook his head. "Nope," he said. "It's on a section of school land, all right—but one old German went down and tried homesteading it and finally gave up. He couldn't stand it. No man in his right mind would try homesteading down there, anyway. Too lonesome!"

I was getting excited. "You mean it's open now?"

"I reckon so," the man answered. "If there's any man fool enough to live on it."

The man didn't know it, but he was talking to just such a fool.

I went back to my room and tried to consider the thing calmly, but it was too late. In spite of all the overwhelming disadvantages the man had pointed out, he had promised my returned health. I knew I had to have that hot springs property.

I knew I ought to go look at the land before I filed on it and that I should talk the thing over with Bessie first. But now that I had made up my mind, I couldn't wait. If I took what I knew to be only proper precautions, I'd lose days and weeks, maybe months. And now that the property was coming to mean so much to me, I began to be obsessed with the fear that someone else would feel the same way about it and file before I did. No, I couldn't wait. I had to file on it now.

I rushed out of my room and headed down the cow-town street toward the surveyor's office. I did pause on the way a time or two to make further inquiries. At a bank and at a couple of stores, I got the same stories. Nobody questioned the curative powers of the springs; but everyone felt that they were too far away from civilization ever to prove of financial value. The land itself was considered to be worth very little.

I listened, made myself weigh and consider each answer, but the urge to file on the land kept mounting inside me.

The county surveyor was a big man, a typical westerner. Playing it cautious, I asked him about various sections of school land, hoping to cover my eagerness to file on the land with the spring. The surveyor described the sections indifferently until I asked if there was any open land fronting the Rio Grande. Then he came alive.

"There's a good piece down at the mouth of Tornillo Creek," he said. "I recently ran a survey on it—Section 50, Block G17, GCSF Railway, which includes the mouth of the creek. Got a hot spring on it."

He turned to his maps with a sigh. "Wanted to file on it myself," he said, "but my wife wouldn't listen to it. Said I needn't expect her to live in a godforsaken place like that for three solid years."

I took one look at the map, located the mouth of Tornillo Creek, made certain of the location of the hot spring, and said: "I'll give you ten dollars to fill out filing papers for me on that section and these two near it."

Legally, I could have filed on a full complement of eight sections. It was listed as mineral and grazing land and priced at a minimum of $1.50 an acre. But right then I didn't need to be gambling any more money on land. I submitted a bid of $1.61 an acre on the section with the spring, but only bid the minimum on the other two sections. These bids were opened and passed on every day in Austin, with the land going to the highest bid submitted at the time of the opening.

The first payment on the land was to be sent in with the bid, but there was a liberal forty-year loan available at three percent interest. I took the loan and figured my payment. It came to seventy-three dollars and seventy-six cents.

I paid the surveyor his ten dollars, but he told me they wouldn't accept a check for my bid in Austin. I'd have to send a money order. That meant I had to go back to town to find someone who would cash a check for me before I could buy my money order.

I walked back to town, fearful that nobody would want to cash the check of a total stranger. I didn't know a soul in the country, and as I walked along, I began to worry. I knew I'd hesitate to cash a stranger's check. I stood around awhile, wondering where to start. Finally, I stopped a big tall lanky cowhand who strolled toward me, his spurs clanking on the sidewalk. I told him who I was and asked him where he thought would be my best chance of cashing a check.

He looked me over carefully, chewed the corner of his underlip a moment, then said: "Why, hell, make out your check. I reckon I can cash it."

Just to look at him in his shabby, half-dirty riding clothes, you wouldn't have suspected he had the price of a drink on him. But he reached down into his hip pocket to withdraw a flattened roll of greenbacks big enough to choke a mule. While I wrote out the check, he licked a thumb and carefully peeled off seventy-three dollars in greenbacks, then dug around in his pocket till he found the extra seventy-six cents.

I was too startled to thank him properly, but he didn't seem interested, anyhow. He just said, "Yeah, sure," and stuffed my check in his pocket and went on down the street, dragging his heavy spurs.

I never saw the man again.

I went back to the county surveyor's office, picked up my filing papers, then hurried to the postoffice to get my money order. But when I got there, the postoffice was closed.

I began to feel panicky. I was filled with a pushing, driving urge to get this thing settled right away. I was afraid to lose a minute. Soon it would be train time, and here I was, unable to get the papers off on that train.

I hunted up the postmaster, L. W. Derrell, and he gladly went back down to the postoffice with me and issued me the money order. Once again, I was impressed by how cheerfully the citizens of this little West Texas cow-town went to all sorts of extra trouble to accommodate a stranger.

When the train came through from El Paso that night, I was at the depot, standing ready to hand my letter to the mail clerk.

Two weeks later, back in Midland, I received my award card. As soon as I could then, I packed up our furniture and even our buckboard for shipment by rail to Alpine. My team I sold there in Midland, and that was the last that buckboard was to see of a team of its own.

And now, here we were, bound for our claim on the Rio Grande.

Beside me, Lovie sat up suddenly. "Look at the birdies, Daddy," she called excitedly, pointing. "Look at the little running birdies!"

I looked in the direction she pointed. "Quail, baby," I said. "Blue quail!"

We were right on them, but the slate-blue birds with their tiny white topknots didn't fly. They merely ran and scattered, uttering little querulous cries, and melted from sight into the grass.

The wheels of the wagons rumbled over the rocky road. Juan Salas woke up enough to shout vigorous commands at his slow-traveling burros, who paid no attention to him whatever. Astride the mare, Enrique broke into a plaintive Mexican song that seemed somehow—although I could understand none of the words—to express exactly what I felt about this vast, strange and silent land that seemed to swallow us as quickly as the brush and grass had swallowed the quail.

Two

BY MID-AFTERNOON of that first day, we had traveled only about ten miles when the burros came to a halt. I looked up in surprise. We had been winding between hills listing sharply on either side. And now the rimrocks glowed with an opalescent light under the slanting rays of the afternoon sun. It couldn't possibly be past four o'clock.

But the indications were obvious. Juan was leisurely climbing down from the freight wagon and slowly unharnessing the burros. Apparently, we were already pitching camp for the night.

I protested vigorously. I pointed out to Juan that we had at least three more hours of daylight. I told him that it was a long way to our claim on the Rio Grande, that we were anxious to get there, and that if we stopped this early every day, it would take us at least a week to make the trip.

To all of this, Juan, who could not understand a word of English, bowed and smiled politely and continued to unharness the burros.

Enrique slid from the back of the belled mare and stooped to put rawhide hobbles on her forelegs. He stripped her of saddle and bridle, then slapped her on the rump. Finally, he turned stiffly and explained in his sketchy English, with obvious contempt at my ignorance. It was the burros, he said; they had pulled the wagons as far as they would go today. Enrique didn't bother to enlarge on the subject, and I still didn't understand.

I was to become much better acquainted with burros before I left this country. In fact, I was to own one myself before I caught onto the curious fact that man's enslavement of the typical Mexican burro can go only so far and no farther. The burro reserves certain personal rights of his own.

For instance, he will pull and carry monstrous loads for man; but always on his own terms. Those terms being that he travel his own pace, that he carry or pull not one pound more than what he considers his full load, and that when he is ready to stop for the day, he stops. Man, with his superior intellect, can devise all sorts of ingenious methods of torture in an effort to get more work out of the little animal, but it's all wasted. When a burro's mind is made up, man may as well accept that fact gracefully. Man may kill the burro, but he'll not change the animal's mind.

My protests coming to nothing, I helped Bessie and Lovie down from the buckboard. We stood and watched till the harness was removed from the last burro and he was free to trail after his teammates. They all followed devotedly after the mare as she grazed toward a grass-filled box canyon that fronted on the camp site.

I wondered some at releasing the burros in such a manner. What was to keep them from straying away, leaving us and our wagons stranded out here in the foothills? But I didn't worry about it. The banker in Alpine who'd recommended Juan Salas to me had pointed out that Juan was a regular freighter between Terlingua and Alpine; I supposed Juan must know his business.

As the clanging of the mare's bell moved away from camp, I was struck by the death-like stillness of this new world. There were sounds, of course. There was the sound of the mare's bell. There was the scream of an eagle soaring high in the blue overhead. And near at hand were the peculiar noises of disturbed blue quail, flushed by the browsing burros. Yet, somehow, these were only surface sounds, each one separate, so that they in no way affected the vast, impenetrable silence that hung over the country.

Sight of the quail aroused my hunting instincts. With hours of daylight left, I should be able to shoot a mess for supper.

From the buckboard, I withdrew about the newest thing in shotguns in those days: a twelve-gauge, double-barreled hammerless, put out by the Syracuse Arms Company. It seemed to me then and still does—for I still own the weapon—that that gun could reach out farther, yet damage small game less than any other shotgun I ever used. I was proud of it and proud of my ability to bring down bobwhite quail on the wing with it.

But when I flushed my first birds that afternoon, I was to learn that my skill at wing shooting was of little importance with blue quail. They wouldn't fly; all they'd do was scatter and run and hide.

I thought at first that it was because of Lovie, who followed at my heels, chattering incessantly. Or possibly Tex, Lovie's self-appointed guardian, who persisted in nosing out ahead of Lovie every foot of ground that she was to step on.

By a little maneuvering, I managed to leave Lovie and Tex to one side. But still, the next quail I flushed refused to fly.

There was nothing to do but potshoot the quail on the ground if I was to get any, even if this did offend my sense of sportsmanship. Only now and then did I get a wing shot; but that was after I'd first shot into the birds on the ground.

There were blue quail in those hills by the thousands in those days, and it was no time before Lovie and I were back in camp with plenty for supper. The Mexicans, Juan and Enrique, had no guns and were delighted at the prospect of a quail supper.

I turned the birds over to Bessie, then set out to find wood for cooking. And that's when I got my third lesson for one afternoon.

We had stopped at an old camp site and there was no wood in sight; no wood of any size, that is. Just bits of agerita brush, and the dead bloom stalks of the sotol plant. And here and there the ocotillo, a strange desert plant that lifted its thorny branches like the groping arms of an octopus. When I examined the plant closer, I found a fresh scarlet bloom in the top of each branch, although the main branches looked dead enough to burn.

I returned to camp, carrying a skimpy load of dead brush that I felt sure would flare up, burn fiercely for a moment, then die away before the heat could possibly cook anything.

Juan and Enrique looked up from helping Bessie clean the quail, caught sight of my firewood, and grinned. Juan rose, dragged a grubbing hoe from his wagon, and strode out to the edge of camp, where he started digging around a dead mesquite shrub whose base was hardly bigger than my wrist. In a moment, he was working away from his starting point, as if intent on digging a crooked trench in the ground.

I moved closer and found this to be the case; he was digging a trench. But down in the trench was the root of the dead mesquite shrub, much larger and heavier than I would have believed.

Following the root out till it became too small to be of any use, Juan reversed his grubbing hoe and used the bit to chop the root free at both ends. Stooping, he dragged from its earthen bed a long stick of wood worthy of being carried to any camper's fire.

That was my first experience in having to grub for wood.

We ate as the sun dropped behind the hills, setting fire to the ragged peaks at first, then dying out to leave an afterglow of vivid coloring.

The silent night closed in. Bessie and I kicked aside a few loose rocks on the level ground near the wagon and made down our bed—a mattress thrown down onto a spread-out wagon sheet, with sheets over the mattress. We didn't bother with quilts; the night was too warm.

The Mexicans each lifted a tattered and dirty blanket from the wagon and moved out into the darkness beyond the firelight.

Lovie, silent at last, slept between Bessie and me; and Tex curled up on the ground as close as she could get to the mattress. Tex slept fitfully between periods of rising with a low growl to go investigate some strange scent that might mark the approach of an imagined danger.

Along about midnight, a spatter of rain aroused us. We got up to move our bed in under the wagon. After that, I lay awake for a time, listening to the weird singing of the coyotes among the hills, thinking of the venture ahead of us.

Bessie stirred in the darkness and I wondered again if I'd done the right thing. Was I risking her life when I made the decision to come out here? Back in Midland, I had gone by and had a long talk with Dr. W. W. Lynch; he had given me full instructions on taking care of Bessie, should the baby come before we could get a doctor. Still, I was no doctor; I wouldn't be able to help Bessie if there were any complications with the birth.

She stirred again, and I knew she was awake. "Bessie," I called softly. "Did I do the right thing? Do you think we'll make a go of it, or have I just made a mess of everything?"

Bessie answered quietly, but with confidence in her voice: "Oscar, I think we're all going to love this country. And I just have a feeling you're going to get well out here."

That was Bessie. If she ever had a doubt about my ability to take care of her and the children, she never let me know it.

I turned over and went back to sleep.

Three

I AWOKE AT DAYLIGHT that second morning to find the sober and aloof Enrique building up the campfire, while Juan Salas squatted on his heels, slashing away a sotol plant with a huge knife.

With clean, efficient strokes, but with the leisureliness that was his way of life, Juan cut away the saw-edged blades of the sotol, leaving a stool about the size of a large cabbage head, with a faint resemblance to a pineapple. This he placed in a hole he dug in the ashes, heaped the ashes over it and, once the fire was well started, dragged red coals over it all.

Noting my curiosity, he exposed his smooth white teeth in a friendly smile.

"*Bueno para comer!*" he said, going through a quick pantomime of eating something most delectable.

Both Mexicans then squatted there beside the campfire in an attitude of waiting, while Bessie and I arose and prepared our breakfast of hot biscuits, fried bacon, and coffee. When we offered to share with the Mexicans, they accepted small portions of our food with polite nods and murmurs of thanks. But even as they ate, their attention was centered on the coals heaped over their roasting sotol stool.

We were finished with breakfast and Bessie was washing our few dishes when Enrique looked a question at Juan and Juan nodded. Enrique poked a stick into the coals and dragged the smoking sotol from the fire.

In its scorched and blackened state, the sotol resembled nothing I thought I'd want to eat. But with a quick slash of his knife, Juan halved the head there on the ground, revealing its yellow-brown core, around which the flesh was bound in tight layers like that of an onion.

Without waiting for the food to cool, Juan and Enrique tore away the outer layers of each half, slapping their scorched fingers against their thighs to cool them. Once the burnt sotol layers had been discarded, the Mexicans matched our politeness by tearing off inside layers of the plant and presenting them to Bessie and me.

Bessie had just passed the morning-sickness stage, and I saw her get a little white around the mouth; but I saw no polite way of refusing the food. We took it and bit into the coarse, fibrous plant. I was watching Bessie closely; but in a moment, the color came back into her face. She looked at me with a grin of reassurance. We found the plant definitely edible, with a peculiar scorched sweetish flavor; but it wasn't anything either of us. would go to any trouble to get. I was thankful, at least, that Bessie was able to eat it without getting sick.

I was to learn later that while most Mexicans did not seem to be as fond of roasted sotol as these two, still all of them ate it at times. Furthermore, I was to learn that many creatures in the Big Bend fed on sotol—black-tail deer, black bear, antelope, cows, mustang horses, burros, and even sheep and goats, when ranchers helped them get at the core of the plant. And some ranchers still consider the sotol bloomstalk, while it's in the bud stage, to be the best available plant food for producing milk in livestock.

Breakfast done, Enrique wandered off through the lush grass and flowering cacti toward the sound of the gray mare's bell. And I learned some more about Mexican burros. When Enrique came riding back on the mare in a few minutes, I was astonished to see all the burros, instead of being driven, trailing dutifully along behind the mare.

Why did they follow her? That one I can't answer yet. But along the Rio Grande there, it is taken for granted among the natives that you must have a belled mare as their leader if you want to handle a bunch of burros, and that, once they have centered their devotion on her, a dozen mounted men and a shepherd dog couldn't keep them away from her for any length of time.

As Enrique led the burros into camp, Juan tied the end of a fifty-foot rope to a front wheel of the wagon, then walked to the end of the rope and held it about waist high at right angles to the wagon. Enrique rode close, then swung back to circle his burros. With a shout, he startled them into a run, right into the outstretched rope. Before they could whirl away or back out, Juan, with a sudden and unexpected burst of energy, dashed around them with the rope, holding them in a tight group against the wagon.

The burros could have escaped. All they had to do was to slip under the rope or jump it. Yet, for no explainable reason, the instant the rope touched them, they stopped stock still and waited for Enrique to bring the bridles and slip the bits into their mouths.

Curious creatures, the burros of this country.

We moved out again, as we had the morning before, with Enrique leading the procession astride the gray mare, traveling at about the same pace as an old-time funeral procession. The grass-covered, flower-studded hills rose about us. We'd head into a valley that seemed to have no possible outlet, travel till the hills seemed to move in behind us, cutting us off from any possible retreat. Then, just as we appeared trapped for good, the hills ahead would suddenly stand aside, leaving room for the two ruts of our road to pass through.

As the sun climbed higher, the green grassed slopes began to shimmer in the heat. Never have I seen such grass as grew in West Texas in those days. Endless miles of it stretched out in every direction. It stood knee-deep to a horse everywhere, and wherever there was room for a grass plant to grow, there one grew. Clear up to the tops of the highest ridges it grew, almost hiding the glistening rimrocks; and down on the slopes and in the valleys, only the tallest of the desert plants stood out above it.

Looking at it then, it seemed to me that there was enough grass growing in the Big Bend country to fatten every horse and cow in the United States. I knew none of the names for the various types of grass I saw; but as we moved deeper into the mountains, one type, a bunch grass that I later learned to call "chino," began to displace all others.

I wondered if I would have such grass on my three sections.

It was along in the middle of the morning that we got our scare. We had crossed a deep, rough draw with a trickle of water running through. And as we came out onto level ground just beyond, we heard a sudden pound and clatter of hooves and looked up the valley to see a herd of some twenty cows and calves come stampeding toward us out of a tall stand of white-brush and catsclaw.

"Oscar, what is it?" Bessie cried.

I stiffened in the springseat. I'd never seen cattle so frightened before. They came tearing out of the brush straight toward us, their eyes wild with fear, their tails standing straight up over their backs.

I thought for a panicky moment that they would rush headlong into the wagons. Juan and Enrique must have thought so too; both began shouting and waving their arms. But at the last mo-

ment, the cattle veered and headed toward the gap between the
burros and the gray mare.

And that's when we saw the panther, or Mexican lion, as he's
called in this part of the country. He was right on the heels of the
cattle, lunging after the last calf with great bounding leaps.

Apparently, he saw us at the same time we saw him, and his
surprise equaled ours. He suddenly checked his charge and slunk
to the ground and held for an instant in an undecided crouch.

How long he stayed there, I'm not sure. For now, everything
was in a wild turmoil. Tex was baying mightily, and Juan was
shouting *"León! León!"* in a terrified voice. Enrique clung to the
back of the gray mare, who was up on her hind legs and walking
in circles. The burros were lunging and braying and trying to kick
out of harness. Bessie was shouting: "Do something, Oscar! Do
something!" And beside me Lovie was screaming her head off.

And down on the floor of the wagon under the springseat was
my shotgun, somehow wedged in such a manner that I couldn't
pull it out. And my rifle was on the ore wagon.

When I finally did get the shotgun out, it was too late. Already,
with a snarl of defiance, the huge cat had wheeled and was bounding back toward the cover of white-brush that he'd come out of.

I sat in stunned silence till he'd disappeared, then turned to
watch the cattle. Less than a hundred yards away, they were still
running wildly, with their tails still standing stiff and straight over
their backs.

The burros were the first to settle down after the excitement.
The mare kept up a fiddle-footed dance under Enrique for almost
an hour. Juan was disturbed, too. He kept clattering away at
Enrique, now and then glancing back over his shoulder appre-
hensively. And Lovie kept standing up in the seat and talking a
mile-a-minute about the "big ugly cat after the poor little calves!"
Even Tex kept bristling up and glancing back in the direction of
the panther.

But the burros evidently operated on an out-of-sight, out-of-mind theory. Once they lost scent of the cat, they quieted down and seemed to lose interest in everything but hauling the wagons along. And at the pace they moved, nobody could rightfully have accused them of having any great and compelling urge to do that.

Four

THAT NIGHT WE CAMPED at old Fort Peña, where in 1881 a band of Apaches had made a last fierce and fatal effort to slaughter the United States soldiers stationed there.

Enrique and I looked the old fort over, but decided against using it for shelter. There were only a few walls of rock and mortar left, and part of the roofs were fallen in. Besides that, it looked too "snaky" for us.

We pitched camp on a piece of level ground across a pond from the fort, and that night after another quail supper, Bessie and Lovie and I had a good splash in the pond.

"Lovie wants to swim," Lovie had announced. In those years, she always spoke of herself in the third person.

Bessie had asked me to see if the Mexicans would leave camp long enough for us to get our swim. But when I explained to Enrique, he couldn't understand such foolishness. And looking at him, from his great drooping straw *sombrero* down to his brogans, it was easy to see that he was not in the habit of bathing regularly.

However, he resigned himself with a shrug of his shoulder and went out to where Juan was digging up a sotol clump and told him what I wanted. Juan turned and smiled at me, nodded courteously, and led Enrique around the point of a hill away from camp. Evidently Juan had been exposed to water at some time in the past.

We splashed into the pool, Lovie jumping up and down and screaming with excitement. Most of the pond was too shallow for swimming, but the bottom was of clean, smooth sand so that we could lie on it and splash around with Lovie and scrub our sweaty bodies to our hearts' content.

I'll always remember that night as the high spot of our trip to the homestead. A cool bath had refreshed us. A supper of biscuits, fried quail and brown gravy had satisfied our appetites. A cool breeze blew down the valley, making our sleep restful. And in the cottonwoods above us, the cries of the Mexican screech owls quavered back and forth across the lake all night long. Their cries were lonely, yet there was in them something pleasantly stirring.

We ate lunch the next day at Garden Springs in the shade of the cottonwoods that stood beside a clear pool. At this point in our trip, the mountains and hills began to shrink in size and stand farther apart, so that we traveled in broad, level valleys. This lengthened the radius of our vision, gave us a better view of the distant rugged peaks, and at the same time increased our feeling of being small, unimportant creatures, lost in a vast, wild land.

We bathed again that night, this time in a long pool of the Maravillas Creek on the Combs ranch. We'd pitched camp at the north end of the lake and then gone swimming. It was here that Lovie spied the ducks. They were sitting on the water at the far end of the lake. She stood up and pointed at them.

"Lovie want duck for supper," she demanded.

Wild duck would be a good change from blue quail, I agreed; but wanting ducks and getting them are two different things.

Lovie wanted to go help me shoot the ducks, but I persuaded her to stay with her mother.

The cover around the edge of the water was sparse and I knew it would take all my skill as a stalker to get within shooting range. I walked in a stooped position behind the brush and crawled in the grass when the brush played out. Weakened as I was by my years of illness, I was in no condition to be stalking game in any such manner. Sweat poured down over my face. My breath gave out, and I had to stop for awhile to get it back.

And whenever I parted the brush to see how close I was getting to the ducks, they seemed farther away than ever. Either I wasn't covering much ground, or else the ducks had got wise to me and were moving on. If it hadn't been for Lovie's complete faith in my ability to get her the ducks for supper, I would have called the whole thing off.

Finally, however, I came to the lower end of the body of water. The ducks had to be there, else I would have seen them when they flew. Yet, when I eased down to the edge of the water, there wasn't a duck in sight.

I couldn't understand it. I came to my feet, feeling an unwarranted sense of frustration and disappointment. Then, suddenly, out of the tall grass almost under my feet, the ducks rose with a squawk and a clatter of wings. They came right up in front of me, so close I could almost have touched them with my gun.

But I was caught too surprised to shoot. When finally I did come to my senses, the ducks appeared beyond the reach of my gun. I lined up on them and fired anyway.

And killed both ducks with that one shot.

Lovie got her ducks for supper; and my pride in myself as a hunter climbed several notches under the warm smiles and broadly gestured praises of Juan, who made it plain in any language that he considered it a miracle that a man could kill two flying ducks with one shot.

There was even a bit of grudging respect for me in the eyes of Enrique, who until now had apparently held a very low opinion of my abilities as a provider.

Slowly the days went by, with only the change in the country distinguishing one day from another. One night we spent at Double Windmills on the bank of the winding Maravillas. Here, two windmills, standing several yards apart, pumped cold water into an earthen tank that had been gouged out of the ground, supplying water for men and their animals in the daytime and for the wild creatures of the desert at night.

A lone cottonwood stood beside the tank, and it was here that I began to appreciate the cottonwood as no other tree I'd ever known before. Partly because it was the only real tree in this country big enough to shade a human being from the hot sun, but even more because its presence marked the water holes.

In this great expanse of country, where water was scarce, a stranger might easily die of thirst if it weren't for the fact that he could climb onto any high rise and spot living water by the presence of the tall, graceful cottonwoods. Wherever the cottonwood grows, there you'll find water.

It was in this section of the country, too, where we first noticed the untold numbers of whirlwinds, or "devil's witches," that moved across the landscape. You would be looking out across a stretch of valley, quiet and serene under the hot sun, when suddenly without warning, a patch of dust would erupt with all the sound and appearance of a small dynamite explosion. And instantly, the dust would form into a tight whirling column that would start moving slowly off across the country, spouting leaves and trash out of its funneled top as it went. Sometimes the columns stood straight and sometimes they were bent and twisted, and often they were so numerous that you grew tired of trying to count them.

I've seen single "devil's witches" in many sections of West Texas, and in several places I have seen as many as a dozen at one time. But never have I seen them in the numbers that we saw them there in the valley of the Maravillas.

During the early hours of our fifth morning out, we started up a gradual incline, the last lap over this great *mesa* spreading from the Maravillas to the Santiago Mountain Range. It was here, headed toward Persimmon Gap, that we came upon the strangest and most beautiful sight of the trip—a forest of flowering sotol.

Along the way, we'd been seeing occasional sotol plants, a relative of the yucca. And it had been a plant worth notice, with its huge stump of glistening light green, wand-like blades, thrusting out in all directions from the base, with its tall bloom stem in the center holding aloft huge clusters of creamy blossoms. Some of these bloom stems were as high as 12 feet.

But here, try to imagine an area eight miles through, where almost nothing grew except flowering sotol. Thousands upon thousands of big white flower clusters, with here and there the sight of deer feeding on the sotol buds. It was breath-taking, like nothing I'd ever before encountered.

As we moved through this sotol stand where the deer fed, it came to me that I might vary our quail and duck diet with a fat buck. I got out my rifle and walked into this strange forest, moving parallel to the wagons about a hundred yards away.

But I got no buck, or doe, or even a fawn. This forest belonged to the deer. They knew it, and I didn't. And although I quite often heard the clatter of the deer's hoofs as they scattered in fright ahead of me, only once did I get a glimpse of one's black tail as he whirled away, too fast for me even to get my gun to my shoulder.

I finally gave up and joined the wagons again, hot and sweaty, and stinging in three different places where the needle-pointed lechuguilla had stabbed me.

"Did you see anything?" Bessie asked as I climbed into the slow-moving buckboard.

I shook my head and showed her a bloody wound in the calf of my leg. "This is all I got. I think we'd better settle for quail or rabbit," I said.

We reached Persimmon Gap, the gateway through the Santiago Range, at late noon, and there we got our first view of the Chisos Mountains.

They lunged up out of the landscape some twenty-five miles away, and their towering peaks, blue and purple at that distance, made a magnificent, awe-inspiring sight. There is a strange, mystic beauty about that mountain range, something compelling and mysterious that grips you the first time you see it and never afterward leaves you.

We ate lunch in the meager shade of the black persimmon shrubs that had given the mountain pass its name. Then, for the next five miles, it was a downhill go, with the hind wheels of our wagons brake-locked and sliding, and the burros forced to move at what must have seemed an alarming pace to them, since sometimes they almost had to trot to keep the wagons from rolling down on the wheelers.

Camp was pitched at Bone Springs that night, the most desolate spot on our journey. Rains had been plentiful on the north side of the Santiagos, but on this side rain had not fallen for nearly three years. What grass the cattle hadn't eaten to the ground was bleached white; and the springs, never strong, were a mere trickle now, proving a fatal trap for the herds of cattle who came to stand around, waiting vainly for a chance to drink.

Too many of them had never got their chance, and now their carcasses lay rotting in the sun, supplying food for the buzzards in the daytime and the coyotes at night. It was a gruesome, foul-smelling place; but it was the only water hole for a good many miles—too long a distance for us to pass it up.

We got little sleep because of the smell and because of the snarls and squallings of the coyotes fighting over the carcasses; and Tex bayed constantly, trying to make it plain that no coyote had better come near our camp.

Bleary-eyed for lack of sleep, we pulled out at the first break of day the next morning. And although we had to cross five miles of this barren waste, where the alkali dust churned up by the burros and the wagonwheels nearly stifled us, nobody complained. We were too glad to get away from that camp site of lurking death.

The dust was the worst in Dog Canyon Flat; but once across it, we moved into a country where the chino grass grew tall again among the many varieties of flowering desert plants.

That night, we camped by an earthen tank on the Dunbar and Wyert homesteads, grateful for the chance to breathe clean air again and to wash the alkali dust from our tired bodies.

Five

AT THE START OF OUR TRIP, I'd been worried about the possibility of spending a full week on the road. And now, on the seventh day, we were still a good twenty miles from our homestead.

That was the day we arrived at the Ira Boggs's ranchhouse. It was a comfortable three-room rock structure built in a grove near a cold spring on the north side of the McKinney Mountains.

Ira Boggs came out to meet us. He was a big red-faced Irishman.

"Come in! Come in!" he shouted. "Light down out of that buckboard and come in this house!"

His wife came out, too, and asked us in. It was plain that these two saw few people. Their welcome was almost pathetic, and again I wondered if Bessie would be able to stand the loneliness.

We went in and visited with the Boggses awhile. When we started to go, they begged us to stay over with them for a few days.

"It'll give you all a little rest," Mrs. Boggs said.

I looked at Bessie. She did look tired. Dark circles had formed under her blue eyes, and her face looked drawn. Lovie, too, looked worn out. Maybe I was succumbing to the Mexican's attitude toward time, but as anxious as I was to get to our new property, I decided that a visit with these people would do us all more good than that same amount of time spent on our own land.

Boggs, with the aid of Mexican herders and dogs, ran a big herd of Spanish goats on his claim. In the cool of the evening, when the herders were bringing the goats in off the range to suckle their young and then bed down near the house, Boggs led me out to give me my first look at the colorful animals.

There were hundreds and hundreds of goats, some white, some black, some blue-and-white spotted, some brown, some mouse colored, some spotted with tan—almost every conceivable combination of colors. Long goatees of hair hung from the chins of the billygoats, giving them the look of sardonic old men; and from the jaws of many nanny goats and billies drooped little wattles of hair that flicked about like the ear pendants women wear.

The herders drove them from the rear, hurling stones to one side or the other of the leaders. Usually such warning was enough, but if the goats failed to turn, the herders sent one of the dogs in. The dog would go flashing through the brush to attack the rebel goats with mock savagery that quickly became genuine if the goats refused to turn.

As I stood watching the herds approach, I became aware of plaintive bleating sounds nearer at hand. Turning, I saw a startling sight. All around me, in the cracks of rocks, in the shade of almost every shrub, I found young kid goats coming to life. And every one of them was bleating frantically and struggling against a forefoot tied into the fork of a stick that had been driven into the ground.

"What's this?" I demanded of Boggs.

Boggs grinned. "That's the way you have to tie a goat kid," he explained. "Tie him around the neck, like you would anything else, and he'll choke himself to death."

[31]

"But why tie them at all?" I asked. "Why not let them go with their mothers?"

"Can't," Boggs said. "When the little devils get full of milk, they always want to lie down and go to sleep. Then the herd grazes off and the coyotes and eagles come along and eat them."

I watched while the herds broke up, the mother goats seeking out their young. The herders came and started releasing the tethered kids. With great stamping and hunching and wiggling of their short, sprightly tails, the kids attacked their mothers' udders for the milk to fill their bellies. Lovie came out to watch, too, and was fascinated. She played with the goats till dark, when we had to lead her, protesting, away to bed.

That night, sleeping in a comfortable bed in Boggs's home, we heard a baby crying out in the dark. Bessie was the first to hear it. In alarm, she shook me awake.

"Oscar," she said. "Listen! I hear a baby crying somewhere!"

"You're just hearing things," I told her.

"You listen," she insisted.

I listened. Sure enough, from somewhere out in the brush came the whimpering cry of a baby.

I got up, pulled on my boots, and slipped outdoors to listen again.

The moonlight lay like silver over the mountains and the broad valley. From far off came the lonely, wavering wail of a coyote. And then I heard it again, that sharp cry of a baby in distress.

I rushed toward it, filled with a strange wonder and sort of terror at the thought of a baby crying out here in the night. Whose was it? How did it get here?

At the edge of a heap of rock, I found my "baby" and suddenly felt so foolish that I sneaked back into the house, taking every precaution now not to wake our hosts.

Bessie was out of bed and halfway to the door when I came into the room. She said in a frightened voice: "Did you find it, Oscar? Did you find the baby?"

"*Sh-h-h-h-h!*" I cautioned. "I found the baby, all right. The baby goat, just getting itself born!"

I'm sure our new friends the Boggses would have enjoyed that joke tremendously—if Bessie and I had ever got around to telling them about it.

We stayed two nights with the Boggses, with Bessie bringing our food to the house so that she and Mrs. Boggs could cook and feed us all and wash dishes together.

Juan wanted to stay longer. His burros were beginning to fag; Juan had bought only one hundred pounds of grain to see them through the entire two-hundred-and-thirty-mile round trip. He thought we should lay over several days to give the burros a rest.

It was Boggs who helped me out. Knowing how anxious we were to get home, he told us we could hitch in four of his fresh burros. He said we could release them once we reached the Rio Grande, and it wouldn't be but a week or two till they came back to his place. It turned out to be two months before the burros returned, but we had no way of knowing that at the time.

We accepted Boggs's offer gratefully and were soon on our way again.

Six

AT NOON ON THE TENTH DAY of our long trip, after having wound over miles of rough mountain road, we arrived at Boquillas, Texas, or La Noria, "The Well," as the village was sometimes called. It was situated a few hundred yards east of Tornillo Creek and comprised a store, a school building, and some ten adobe cabins. There were several *jacales,* or huts, made of sotol and maguey bloom stalks, with ocotillo roofs on which clay was laid about six inches thick.

Our approach was heralded by the savage barking of many mongrel dogs and the squawking of colorful Spanish chickens as they fled to safety behind the cabins. Little brown dusty-footed children stood out in the street and stared at us curiously as we drew up in front of the store.

The storekeeper and postmaster, J. R. Landrum, came out to welcome us to the Big Bend country and to invite us to lunch with him in the coolness of his store building. We were happy to accept.

"Just take it easy, here in the shade, till the cook gets dinner ready," he told us.

We took it easy, entertaining ourselves by watching the coming and going in the village. Most of the group hanging around the store were Mexicans, Texas pioneer ranchmen, and their new homesteading neighbors. All spoke in voices peculiarly soft and gentle, which seemed characteristic of this country, and the conversations were generally held in Spanish.

Of them all, the Mexicans were the most colorful. They came riding up to the store astride Spanish ponies or burros so small that often the riders' feet were almost touching the ground. They wore grand *sombreros,* red bandana handkerchiefs around their necks, flashy shirts, fancy *sarapes* around their waists, and skin-tight buckskin trousers flared at the bottom. A few wore deerskin moccasins.

Some drove burros loaded with root wood, and others had their beasts so loaded with freshly cut chino hay that only the little animals' ears stuck out.

They came and tied their burros at the hitching rail in front of the store, squatted on their heels to talk and smoke corn-shuck cigarettes awhile in the shade, then mounted and rode off.

We ate, with Landrum telling us some about the country and the customs of the gentle people who live here.

In a pause in the conversation, Bessie asked Mr. Landrum how he happened to come to Boquillas.

Landrum looked at Bessie a moment, then finally said: "I came from Florida, Mrs. Langford. I had a law practice there; but when I developed consumption, the doctors told me to move west. I was living at Alpine when Ernst, the man who owned this store, was murdered last year. His family asked me to be executor of the estate, and—well, I just stayed on."

I wasn't liking this turn of the conversation. It was too gloomy, and I didn't want Bessie to get a depressing picture of life here before we'd even seen our own property. But Landrum went on to tell about the killing.

"Funny thing about Ernst," he said. "He was peace officer here, besides being storekeeper and postmaster; but he wouldn't wear a gun. Wouldn't let the white settlers carry a gun, either. He was a friendly man and the Mexicans liked him; he felt great confidence in their friendship and always said it was wrong to go around armed among such friendly people. But it was Mexicans that murdered him.

"There's no postal service across the river," Landrum continued, "so the natives of Mexico over there use this Texas postoffice. One day a check sent through this postoffice from the Mexican side turned out to be bad, and Ernst was sent to investigate.

"He was returning," Landrum went on grimly, "with papers that were rumored to prove the Mexicans fraudulent. And as he rode through a gap in the mountains, he was ambushed. Shot in the stomach. He didn't die immediately, but rode on to the house of a friend, Clemente Mena. There, he died late that night."

"Did they ever find out who did it?" I asked.

Landrum shook his head. "Ernst never would tell," he said. "He refused to make a statement about the attack on him or about the fraudulent check. He just kept saying, 'I can talk to them. I can straighten the thing out.' Even against these Mexicans that killed him, Ernst was unwilling to let any white man but himself bring justice."

I looked at Bessie. She looked pale and frightened. Suddenly I was so anxious to get on the road again that I could hardly finish my meal and say goodby to Landrum quickly enough.

"Wonder how far we are from my piece of land," I asked him.

"About seven miles," he said.

"Why, if we drove fast," I exclaimed, "we might get there tonight!"

Landrum smiled at my impatience. "You might," he said, "if you had a team that you could drive fast. There's some mighty rough country between here and there."

Seven

LANDRUM WAS RIGHT. We didn't make it there by night. The narrow road leading away from Boquillas lasted for only about a mile before swinging off southeast toward the mines at Boquillas, Mexico, across the Rio Grande. From there on, all we could do was follow down the stream bed of Tornillo Creek as it wound deeper and deeper between high, brown, crumbling canyon walls toward its mouth at the Rio Grande. Past floods had littered the stream bed with boulders and thrown up deep bars of loose sand.

Over these boulders and through the sand, the little burros plodded along with our wagons, working later than they ever had before, as if they, too, were eager to reach the end of the journey.

Then, on our own land, and less than a mile from the spring, we started across a sand bar so deep that the wagons sank in almost to the hubs. And right there, the burros called it off for the day.

Juan swore and lashed them with a long whip that until now he'd only cracked over their heads. I got down and put a shoulder to a wagon wheel and pushed with all I had. Bessie got out to watch us, and Lovie came and put her tremendous strength to pushing. Lovie was a great help.

Enrique came to help Lovie and me. Juan swore and lashed the burros some more. But nothing came of it. The burros had decided it was quitting time. They were done for the day.

I was badly disappointed, and I could see that Bessie was. But she just looked at me and shrugged her shoulders. "Well, we're on our own land, anyway," she said.

"Sure," I told her, to cover my own disappointment. "And even if we'd got to the river, it's too late for us to start putting up our permanent camp. This way, we'll have all day tomorrow to get unloaded."

But the next morning we were in for another disappointment. When Juan hitched up his team and cracked his whip over their backs, the little burros strained against their collars with all they had and still couldn't move the embedded wagons. I pushed, and Enrique pushed, and Juan said some things in Spanish that nobody could mistake for compliments. But it was no use. Juan finally turned to me, hunched his shoulders, lifted and spread his hands expressively. We were stuck.

I stood and wondered what to do. Juan sat on the wagon and let me wonder. So did Enrique. Without saying a word, they made it plain that the whole thing was beyond them and that, furthermore, if anybody was going to worry about the situation, it would have to be me.

While I stood, trying to figure the thing out, I saw an umbrella of smoke rising from the brush further down the creek. I learned from Enrique that the smoke came from the fire of one Cleofas Natividad, who lived with his family in a dugout in the side of the hill.

"What's he doing living on our land?" Bessie wanted to know.

In a voice that indicated how patient he was trying to be, Enrique explained that Cleofas Natividad was farming some of the land and running a herd of goats on the rest.

Bessie looked at me. I looked back at her. But neither of us said anything. For there really wasn't anything to say. This was a situation neither of us had expected to encounter and we'd nothing in our backgrounds to tell us how to handle it. Involuntarily, I thought of Ernst and his trouble with the Mexicans.

Like most men, I dreaded trouble. I shrank from the idea of having to try to run a Mexican squatter off my land. Still, I needed help. And apparently the only possible help within walking distance was at the campfire.

Reluctantly, I turned and started walking down the creek bed toward the umbrella of smoke. Before I reached it, I could see that the Mexican squatter had cleared something like ten acres of land between the stream bed of Tornillo Creek and the abrupt hills rising beyond. Corn, beans, squash and melons grew in the patch of cultivated ground. I found a ditch leading from the creek toward this cleared land. No water ran in it; in fact, right now the level of the small trickle of water in the creek bed was several feet below the entrance to the ditch.

This puzzled me at first; then I saw what my squatter had in mind. The irrigation ditch was used only in time of floods, when the water rose sufficiently high in the creek bed to spill over into the ditch.

Concerned as I was with having a squatter so entrenched on my land, I had to admire the man's ingenuity. For Tornillo Creek was some sixty miles long, and I was sure that quite often it flooded when no rain fell at this end. No doubt the man was able to irrigate several times a year, even though not always just when he might wish to.

At the edge of the clearing, I saw a number of spotted Spanish goats, such as those I'd seen at the Boggs ranch, grazing in the tall grass and brush. And somewhere nearby, although I could not see them, I caught the sound of laughing, playing children, and the barking of dogs.

Reluctantly, I headed toward the dugout, whose thatched and mud-covered roof I could now barely see above the brush.

But luck was with me, and I didn't have to go ask a favor of a man who could easily turn out to be my enemy. I happened to glance down the creek, and here came a couple of men walking toward me, talking and laughing as they came.

I turned and walked down the creek to meet the strangers. They were Tom Shackelford and his son-in-law, Earl McKinney, who had come with their families from Marathon to bathe at the hot spring. They were camped at the mouth of Tornillo Creek, and right now the two men were walking up the creek, looking for Indian arrowheads.

After we'd introduced ourselves, I explained my predicament with the bogged wagons. Right away, they offered to go back to their own camp and bring up a wagon and buggy to carry our household belongings out and lighten the load on Juan's burros.

We found Juan and Enrique smoking in the shade of the wagon and waiting with relaxed indifference when we got back to our bogged wagons with Shackelford's empty ones. Shackelford was alarmed when he saw that we had bedded down in the middle of the dry creek bed the night before.

"You don't know how lucky you are," he said. "That creek might have flooded last night. I've seen a wall of water four and five feet deep come rampaging down this canyon when there wasn't a cloud in sight. Bringing down boulders big as cotton bales."

I felt a little foolish. I should have known better than to camp there, but I just hadn't thought. There was much I needed to learn about living in this country.

Shackelford and McKinney helped me load most of our cargo

into their wagon, and Bessie and Lovie got into the buggy. Juan climbed slowly back into his wagon and Enrique mounted the gray mare and rode her out in front of the burros. Juan lifted his voice and swore at the little animals. And, with Shackelford and me at the front wheels, they got the wagons rolling again.

Shackelford seemed to take an interest in our homesteading project. He advised us to pitch our camp, for the time being, in a sharp bend of the creek. He pointed out the advantages of a cove on a bench of land above the creek's highwater mark. On two sides were rock-studded cliffs, so that for most of the hot part of every day the cliffs shaded the camp. Just below, a bold stream of water gushed from the creek sand and spilled over rock ledges into a series of bright clear pools. The pools extended all the way to the Rio Grande, which we could just glimpse around the shoulder of the cliff to the south.

"We're camped at a prettier place," he said, pointing to some tall, shady cottonwoods at the mouth of the creek. "But that would be too close to the river for you to stay there with your baby."

Bessie and I agreed with him.

Both men stayed to help us unload and get a tent up; then they took their wagon and buggy back to their own camp, after first inviting us to eat with them.

"Caught us a sixty-pound catfish last night," McKinney said proudly. "We're fixing to fry it and eat fish till the world looks level."

Eight

THIS WAS OUR LAND!

After days of waiting to know if our bid was accepted, and days of packing and getting ready to leave Midland, and finally, after making the long journey through this strange country, we were on our own land, at last.

We stood and stared about us, too excited to do more than make a pretense of getting our camp set up. The rock cliffs towered above us, more than a hundred feet high, their faces great walls of smooth stratified slabs of limestone some six inches thick, with thin layers of clay between.

Across the creek, the hills rose almost as high as the walls behind us, but the slopes were less precipitous. The hills were covered with a thick growth of flowering lechuguilla, sotol, grease-wood, prickly pear, and various other types of cacti, such as the pitahaya. A gentle breeze moved up the canyon, bringing to our ears the muffled roar of the rapids of the Rio Grande.

I looked at Bessie, and she laughed. "All right," she said. "Let's go look at the spring. Then we'll come back and set up camp."

I took Lovie by the hand. Tex led the way. We walked down the bed of the creek, waded a shallow place to the other side, and there got our first glimpse of the wide-rolling Rio Grande and the tumbling sweep of mountains rearing high against the skyline in Mexico.

We came out onto the point of land where the Shackelfords were camped under the cottonwoods. The smell of frying catfish was in the air. Tom Shackelford waved to us.

"You're a little early yet," he said with a grin. "But it's just as well to get set for the big rush when the first piece of fish comes out of the pan."

We told him we wanted to go see the spring first and he said that would be fine, but for us not to stay too long.

"I can't guarantee to keep the womenfolks and the children fought off this fish all day," he shouted.

Tall cane grew beside the river, and above the cane rose more high cliffs. However, a narrow sandy trail led between the cliffs and the cane and we followed it, impatient to see the spring on which we'd counted so strongly.

But less than a hundred yards down the trail, we were stopped again, this time by a swarm of Mexican cliff swallows swooping back and forth across an undercut cliff. There where the sun could not strike the walls, the birds had stuck scores of mud nests to the face of the rock. And from a little hole in the center of each nest protruded the heads of the tiny fledglings, crying loudly for food.

The parent swallows worked frantically to fill the crops of their hungry young. On sharply tipped wings, they flew up from the river canyon at incredible speed, bringing worms or bugs and flying unerringly toward the one little hole, among the scores of little holes, that held their own young. Sometimes they'd hurtle viciously into one another and fall ten or fifteen feet before recovering their balance. And at each encounter, they ruffled their feathers and screeched threats and warnings at each other; but they never stopped feeding their young long enough to fight it out.

I think Lovie would have stood there and watched them all day if we hadn't moved her along. "We'll come and watch them again," I promised her, and led the way on down the twisting trail toward the spring.

It's difficult to tell how I felt when we finally reached it. I'd thought of that spring so much, hoped so fervently that it would give me back the health I'd not had since I was a child.

And now, here it was, boiling up out of a smooth, level ledge of rock.

Up through a hole some six inches in diameter and almost perfectly round, spurted the sparkling water with a force that lifted the column almost a foot above the ledge before it tumbled back in a wreath of white foam.

The apex of the stream looked very much like the crown of a cowboy's hat, and the water spread out around it in a solid sheet to form the brim. From there, it poured off a lip of rock and into the casket-like bathtub that the Indians had built sometime in the past by chipping out and enlarging a fissure in the flat layer of sedimentary rock. Over the bathtub, some white man had erected a tent to give a bather privacy.

Bessie got down on her hands and knees and leaned over and drank from the top of the column of water.

"How is it?" I asked.

"Good," she said.

It wasn't, really. It was too hot and charged with too many chemicals to be called really good. Yet at that, it didn't taste as bad as some water I'd drunk from wells where people had become so accustomed to it that they thought it was good. I predicted then that once we'd got used to the taste, we'd learn to like it; and this prediction proved true.

I studied the spring, considering its possibilities. With a spring on my own property that flowed 250,000 gallons of water a day and kept a constant temperature of 105 degrees Fahrenheit, there should be some way that a man of ingenuity could cash in on it. There were already a few people, like the man in the Alpine Hotel and the surveyor and the Shackelfords, who knew of the spring and its healing qualities.

"If I erected a bath house," I reflected, "with several tubs in it, I could charge a little for baths."

Bessie laughed at me. "Shouldn't we build us a house to live in first?" she asked.

I paid her no attention. "Old timers have told me that the Indians considered the full treatment to take twenty-one days," I went on. "I could charge ten cents a bath, or two dollars for the full treatment. That wouldn't be hard on anyone, and it would bring us in an income—if we could get enough people interested."

"And for that matter," Bessie said, "don't you think even before we build a house to live in, we should go back right now and set up our camp?"

Nine

WE WENT BACK UP the river canyon, talking and laughing, making our plans. We ate fried catfish and visited with the Shackelfords. We sat in the shade of the cottonwoods and dug our heels into the soft sand and talked about the country, the hunting and the fishing.

Some of the Shackelford women asked Bessie if she wasn't afraid to live down here in this wild border country, among the Mexicans and bandits that might come across the river.

But before Bessie could answer, Shackelford laughed. "No more danger down here than anywhere else," he said. "Sure, there've been a few raids and a few killings in the past. Like the killing of old man Ernst. But people can get killed anywhere. They're getting killed in big cities every day!"

I told Shackelford I had encountered some wild tales about this country in Alpine.

He shook his head. "Pay no attention to that," he said. "There's a man over in Fort Stockton started all that. He wanted to get hold of this spring without having to live out his three homesteading years on it. Told all those stories to scare other folks off."

I was relieved to hear this. The stories had sounded like they were highly colored to me; but still, a man bringing a family into a new country can't help worrying a little.

Juan and Enrique, who had stayed to eat catfish, finally had all they could hold. Together they rose, wiped greasy hands on their pants, and got ready to go. I paid Juan his forty dollars for hauling us down, shook hands with them both, and told them goodby.

But when Bessie and Lovie and I left the Shackelfords' camp about an hour later and returned to start setting up our own, we found that not only were Juan and Enrique still with us, but that they had been joined by a Mexican man, his wife, their ten children, and a number of dogs whose presence infuriated Tex.

The Mexicans arose as we approached. Together we quieted the dogs; then Juan removed his hat and bowed.

"*El Señor* Cleofas Natividad," he introduced grandly, then added: "*El Señor* Langford."

So this was my squatter. I wondered if he was here to make trouble. But before I could think what to do or say, Cleofas Natividad, a squat, heavy man, had removed his hat and bowed just as grandly as Juan. Then, with a flashing smile, he turned and spoke to his wife, a big, fat, dark-skinned woman with soft friendly eyes. At his words, she held out to us the raw quarter of a freshly butchered goat. Beside her stood one of the older girls of the family, holding out a basket of eggs artistically wrapped in corn shucks. Another child held a frying-size chicken.

"She will be friends," Enrique explained, eyeing us warily. "She bring gifts."

This was a situation I didn't know how to handle. Hesitating, I looked around at their friendly, hopeful brown faces watching me. I turned to Bessie.

[48]

But Bessie was ahead of me. Already, she had stepped up and was taking the gifts, thanking the visitors with such warm, smiling appreciation that they didn't need to understand her words.

Great smiles parted the lips of even the children when they saw that their gifts were welcome.

Enrique said: *"El Señor* Natividad, she—how you say?—rent your land?"

Again I was baffled. I wasn't right sure whether this illegal squatter thought he was already renting my land, or if he meant that he would like to rent it.

I frowned, trying to decide what to do. After all, we didn't know the customs here and we didn't want to make enemies unnecessarily. Still, this was my land; I had my papers from Austin to prove it.

And that's when it came to me what a trifling thing a deed to a piece of land was. Here I was, a stranger, with a mere piece of paper, considering whether or not I should allow a family to live on land that had probably been their home for generations.

I looked at Bessie again. She nodded. "Why not?" she asked. "You're not able to work the land yet. And the extra money would help."

I nodded to Cleofas. "That will be fine," I said to Enrique. "Tell him that I will be glad to rent my land to him."

The Mexicans all chattered for a moment at a high pitch of excitement, with even the children joining in. Then Cleofas Natividad turned, bowed again, and stuck out his hand. *"Bueno!"* he said, with a wide smile.

I took his hand and shook it.

Enrique said: "She say, tell you, she work for you, pay rent."

The suspicion struck me that if Cleofas was anything like Juan and Enrique, then I'd come out on the short end of this deal. But I could see that I was already too deep in to back out now. I nodded. "That'll be fine," I said, and hoped I was right.

With the deal closed and friendship established, the Mexicans stayed to help us eat the goat and eggs and fryer and all the biscuits Bessie cooked for supper.

Ten

NEAR OUR CHOSEN CAMPSITE was an old abandoned dugout, with its rock walls in an excellent state of repair. Over this, I stretched one of our tents, then erected the other just out in front. This gave us a two-room dwelling, one for sleeping quarters and storing our furniture, the other for setting up our dining table.

Once this was done and a little brush cleared away from the tents, we stopped all work and just rested for several days. We all needed it. Even Lovie was beginning to run down, so that she slept most of that first day.

It was the first real rest I'd had in years. In the mornings, I'd go down to the spring and drink some of the hot water; then I'd bathe in the tub the Indians had built. After a bath, I'd wrap up in a blanket for a good sweat, then wash off again just before leaving.

At first, the baths and sweats weakened me so that for the rest of the day about all I was able to do was to lie around in the shade at camp. And for the first couple of days, the water acted as a mild laxative, weakening me further. But I continued to drink it and take my baths and sweat till I'd finished the full prescribed treatment of twenty-one days. I was determined to give the spring every chance to prove its healing powers.

After a few days, the water seemed to lose its laxative effect, and my appetite increased. Gradually, too, the weakening effect of the bathing and sweating wore off, so that in the cool of the evenings I could go out and shoot quail or rabbits, or prowl the canyons with Lovie and Bessie, just to see what we could see.

What we saw were many things strange to us. Such as the little whitish "button" cacti, so named because they are just about the size and shape of a big coat button. They grew only on the high limestone ridges where there was so little soil that we never quite understood how their roots took hold. We found the star cactus, too, growing so deep in the same rocky soil that its perfect green star in the top was never above the level of the earth. Then there were the tornillo bushes, with their bean pods growing in a screw twist. And the popotillo, a green shrub from which, we later learned, the natives brewed a tea for the treatment of gonorrhea.

We learned to know the beautifully flowering pitahaya, a cactus that produces one of the most luscious fruits of the desert. We watched the doves building their nests in the brush along the river. We grew accustomed to the wailing of the coyotes at night and learned to love the muted sound of the wide-rolling Rio Grande and to note that at night the sound seemed to increase in volume.

We liked to climb to the high places and gaze out over the surrounding countryside, especially in the late afternoons when we could sit and watch the magnificent play of softly tinted colors against the bold battlements of the Carmen Mountains downriver from us in Mexico.

The rattlesnakes we didn't like; for one thing, they prowled only at night when we couldn't see them. It was too hot for them to get out much in the daytime. We learned that there were four different kinds of rattlers in that region: the commonly known diamondback, the lesser known sidewinder, and the almost unknown pink and green rattlers. The latter two are small snakes, seldom seen; and while they're odd enough to be interesting, they're still not the sort of creatures a man wants to seek out as bosom friends.

A six-foot bullsnake took up quarters under our wardrobe that summer. None of us relished the idea, but we let him stay. We'd been told that bullsnakes are deadly enemies of the rattler and are always on the lookout to kill him.

If this story is true, then there was something wrong with our own particular bullsnake. Or he may have just got lazy and gone to sleep on the job. At any rate, Tex woke us up one night with a warning growl, then went to baying frantically. And before I could get a lantern lighted, I heard a rattler sound off, right inside our tent.

You can be sure I lost no time lighting that lantern. We found the snake just inside the door, a six-foot diamondback, coiled and ready to do battle. Tex held him at bay till I could get to my shotgun; then I blew that rattler to meat-scraps.

But if the blast so much as disturbed our bullsnake under the wardrobe, we never knew about it.

However, even though he didn't keep us free of rattlers, we were convinced that our bullsnake did rid the camp of mice and rats. Not once did we discover them in any of our household goods, although we could see their tracks out in the blow sand along the banks of Tornillo Creek.

Actually, the only mice we ever saw were the little kangaroo mice that sometimes came to the light of our campfire at night, apparently drawn as much by curiosity as by the hope of getting anything to eat. They were tiny things with short forelegs, extra long hind legs, and a tail about five inches long with a brush of hair at the end, very much like the brush of a lion. Now and then, we'd throw them a piece of bread or grain and they'd venture quite close to the fire, grab up the food with their short forelegs, then scamper back a way, rearing up on their hind legs and dancing a little dance in perfect rhythm, accented by the waving of their tails.

We liked those little mice and sincerely hoped that our bull-snake never caught any of them.

Our camp lay right on the crooked trail that led from the village of San Vicente, five miles upriver, to the little town of Boquillas, Mexico, some six or seven miles below. Being almost halfway between the two settlements, it proved a convenient stopping-over place for travelers. And it was curious to note how these travelers almost always arrived a little before noon, just in time for a short visit before the food would be served. Usually, we invited them to stay and eat with us, which they did. And thus, we learned later, we did Cleofas a great favor. Until our coming, he'd had to bear the full brunt of feeding these friendly but always hungry way-farers. However, we were always glad to see them, hungry or not, and we came to know them better and to begin to understand them.

We found them a generous, polite people, well satisfied with their way of living. Bessie and I noticed that it was a rare thing when one broke away from his family ties and left home for any length of time. A good many of our new friends had turned down wages as ranch hands beyond anything they could ever hope to earn at home. They turned down those wages in order to live as they wanted to live.

We began to learn, too, something of their customs. For in-stance, when a baby is born, the father gets out his gun and fires it, one shot for a girl, two shots for a boy. He then formally an-nounces the birth to his other children, who usually laugh and kiss and hug each other, then start dancing and shouting, *"El ha venido! El ha venido!"* ("He has come! He has come!")

The marriage customs are unusual. The courtship is short and always carried on in the presence of the father and mother of the *señorita*. When the young man has won the consent of his sweetheart, he has two of his young men friends go with him to her home to ask her parents for their consent to the marriage, which is seldom, if ever, refused.

After he gets their consent, he gives the father enough cash to pay for the trousseau and all the groceries desired by his family until the wedding day, which is usually within two weeks. He then goes back to his home, returning the eighth day with the two friends formally to ask the girl to marry him. The wedding day is set and great preparations are made to entertain the entire settlement.

After the wedding and a feast, and an all-night dance to the music of a string band, the groom takes his bride to the home of his parents. As they approach, the father fires six shots in welcome. They remain with the groom's parents for twenty-four hours, and as they pass out the door on the return to the home of the bride they are showered with rice. They live with the bride's family for three months and then move into a home of their own.

It seemed to Bessie and me that these people made much of life and little of death. They celebrated weddings for days ahead of time. They were overjoyed at births. But they would face the danger of death with a shrug of the shoulder. And the death of a loved one didn't seem to disturb them much. Once a man I'll call Hernando Aguilar stopped by on his way to La Noria. "You know that wife of mine?" he asked. I nodded. "Well," Aguilar said, bursting into a hearty guffaw, "he die las' night."

We found this attitude pretty shocking, at first; but after we'd been in the country long enough, we came to believe that these people accept death as a part of life and not as a thing to concern themselves about unduly.

As the summer wore on, Bessie was unable to go as far as we had gone at first on our exploratory walks. I watched her anxiously.

But, as she seemed to be strong and healthy, I finally decided it was foolish to worry about her condition.

My own health began a steady improvement. I got so I could eat anything. Even for supper, I could eat chili and beans and tortillas, then go right to bed and sleep like a child.

This return of my health was due in part to the quiet and peacefulness of the kind of life I was able to live here in the Big Bend. It was due in part to the relaxed, unworried temperament of the people, which helped me to relax, too. But more than anything else, I felt that I had the healing powers of my hot spring to thank for my return to health.

Bessie and I agreed that if we could prove up on the homestead, every effort toward that would be justified by my renewed health.

When Bessie could no longer go with me, I took to going on long walks by myself. And it was on one of these solitary strolls that I walked right onto a second hot spring not five hundred yards from my own.

This second spring was beyond my property line and, right away I saw what a threat it could be to me and my plans. It came up out of mud and trash, close to the river and wasn't nearly as accessible and pleasant for bathing as mine. But still, there it was, ready to compete for the bathers I hoped to lure to my spring.

The next day I walked to La Noria to find out all I could about this second spring. Landrum, the postmaster, told me the spring was on a section of land owned by a man named G. D. Gordon, who lived at Marion, Iowa. Landrum didn't know if Gordon would lease that land, but he thought he might.

"He's not taking any other income from the property," he observed. "Looks like lease money would be better than no money at all."

As short of cash money as I was, I had no business trying to lease this property. Yet, something had to be done about that spring if I expected to build up the thriving business I'd planned for my own.

That night, I sat down and wrote Gordon a letter, inquiring about a lease and its possible cost.

We were agreeably surprised at the number of visitors who came to camp and to bathe that year. We'd had no idea there'd be so many. And the income we derived from the baths was a great help toward taking care of our living expenses.

Now and then, as I had feared, some of the bathers went to the spring downriver, to avoid paying for their baths. But that spring was almost a loblolly of mud and not nearly so strong or easy to reach as mine. Besides, my rates were not exorbitant; so I didn't have too much trouble.

Nevertheless, the threat that some one would come build up that other spring—cement around it, or pipe the water into tubs— worried me. Time went by, and still I didn't hear from Gordon. I tried to dismiss the thing from my mind and enjoy my visitors.

Of all the guests who came that summer, I think we enjoyed the Harmons most. John Harmon and his sons Clay, Joe, and Charlie came from Alpine. They all took a full course of baths, paying me in advance. And when they weren't bathing, they were fishing.

They were expert fishermen, too; and Bessie and Lovie and I often joined them to learn how to catch the big catfish and buffalo that were so plentiful in the Rio Grande.

We seldom caught a fish under ten pounds that summer; the big ones were eating the little ones, so that the weight of the average catch ranged from twenty-five to fifty pounds. One day we caught a yellow cat that weighed sixty pounds.

To people in town, the cooking and serving of a sixty-pound catfish might present somewhat of a problem. But there, on the river bank, the Harmons managed it with no trouble at all.

First, late in the evening, they built a big mesquite wood fire and let it burn down to a bed of live coals. Then they dragged the coals and ashes aside and dug a trench in the hot dirt. Next they wrapped the fish in a wet gunnysack and put it in the trench and covered it with the hot coals. Then they went to bed.

The next morning, at breakfast time, all they had to do was dig out their fish, unwrap and skin it, shake the meat from the bones, salt and pepper to taste, and go to work on it. Served with hot biscuits and coffee, this baked fish made some of the best eating a man could imagine.

When we caught more fish than we could eat, we staked them out in the deep holes of fresh water in Tornillo Creek. Sometimes we shot fish. During a rise on the Rio Grande, the buffalo and many catfish fed in the shallow backwater of the creek, where it was not so muddy. There, we could shoot and gig all we pleased.

We learned all about fishing that the Harmons could teach us, and continued to enjoy it after they left. For some unaccountable reason, Bessie proved to be the best fisherman of the family. Sometimes it was almost uncanny the way I could sit beside her, fishing with the same kind of hook and the same bait, and watch her pull out one fish after another while I caught almost none.

However, I did manage to land a bigger fish than she ever caught, and do it in a much more spectacular way.

This happened soon after the Harmons had left. A small rise came on the Rio Grande, backing water up into the mouth of Tornillo. The catfish and buffalo moved into the shallow water, as usual. And among them, I spied this whopper of a yellow cat with its fins cutting the surface of the water.

I had no harpoon, such as the Harmons had used. And I was afraid that if I shot the fish, he'd escape to deeper water before I could catch him.

I thought for awhile, studying the fish, then hurried back to camp and improvised a spear out of a long pole, to which I lashed an ancient Confederate bayonet I'd carried with me from home.

Armed with this formidable weapon, I hurried back to the creek. Sure enough, there was my catfish, lying almost still now, as if enjoying a nap in the warm, shallow water. He lay just at the edge of a long sand bar.

Walking carefully, I crossed the sand, lifted my weapon, and with a hard thrust, drove it into his back.

I struck too hard. The bayonet drove completely through the fish. The point struck the flat rock bottom beneath and snapped in two, leaving me with only a few inches of blade still in the fish's back.

I tried to hold that much steel in him as, with a mighty lunge and a great threshing of his tail, he headed for deeper water.

I ran with him, pressing down on my broken weapon with all the strength I could muster. That pressure, holding him against the bottom, was enough to slow his escape, but not enough to stop him. We moved farther and farther out into the river. Blood spouted from the fish's wound and left a red stain in the water behind us.

When finally he gave up, I found myself in waist-deep water some fifty yards out into the flooding Rio Grande.

After resting awhile, I bent and slipped my hand under a gaping gill flap and gripped it tightly. The fish began to struggle again, but I had him now. Pulling with all my strength, I finally dragged him to the water's edge and slid him out onto the wet sand.

His flat head measured exactly twelve inches across, he weighed thirty-five pounds, and when we butchered him, we found inside his stomach the ball of a calf's hip joint. The bone bore the marks of a butcher's saw and, since the nearest butcher shop was at the mining town of Terlingua, sixty miles up the Rio Grande, we were forced to conclude that the catfish had travelled that far in the last day or so, else the bone would already have been digested. Evidently, he had come downriver with the flood.

I had another exciting adventure that summer with a fifteen-year-old boy whose name I have now forgotten.

I'd been up the river rabbit and quail hunting and had discovered a swarm of bees in a cave in a cliff. The cave was out of reach, so that I couldn't look in, but I could tell by the way the bees were working that they probably had honey. Also, I could see the black smoke stain on the rocks around the entrance, which indicated that in the past somebody had been able to rob it.

The chance to get some good wild honey to vary our meals outweighed the hunting. I hurried back to camp, where I improvised a sort of bee veil out of mosquito netting, nailed together a short ladder, and collected pots and pans. Then I started back.

Some bathers were camped at the mouth of Tornillo and, as I came by, this boy saw me and wanted to know if I'd take him along. He said there was nothing he loved better than good wild honey and he promised to help me rob the cave if I'd share the loot with him.

I agreed. He shouldered my makeshift ladder, and we went up the river.

When we arrived at the bee cave, I had the boy set the ladder against the wall and showed him how to hold it in place while I worked.

He was a willing worker—at first. He not only held the ladder, but stood ready to hand me a second dishpan, in case the first couldn't hold all the honey.

I climbed up and looked into the cave opening, which was some eight or ten feet above the ground. The opening was about the size of an apple box, giving me plenty of room to work through. And the honey wasn't far inside. Most of it, hanging in thick rich combs, was stuck to the wall just under the opening, so that all I had to do was reach in with a long-handled camping spoon and start tearing loose the comb and lifting it, dripping, into my pan.

Of course, the moment I went to work, so did the bees. They

were the little black wild bees. And to compare their onslaught with the mild attacks of regular domestic bees would be like comparing a bullet to a spitball. They boiled up out of the hole in a black humming cloud, and they meant business.

With my attention centered on the honey, I forgot about my helper. That is, I forgot about him till I heard a wild yell and felt the ladder go out from under me. Luckily, I had one elbow hooked over the rim of the hole, so that I didn't fall backward. But when I did slip to the ground an instant later, all I could see of my helper was just his bent back, plunging into a tall stand of river cane. The boy was screaming at the top of his voice, and right in after him poured a black cloud of bees.

I finally got my ladder propped up so that it would stand without help and managed to get one panful of good honey before the bees learned how to crawl up my pants legs and in under the cuffs of my shirt.

Then I, too, sold out, and followed the boy through the cane, travelling at about the same urgent speed.

However, I did save that panful of honey. But when I got to camp, the boy wasn't in sight, and he never did come around for his share of the spoils.

Eleven

As my health improved, I began to take more interest in the matter of building us a house. The new baby was expected in November and, although the winters here were said to be exceedingly mild, we still thought it best to have our house ready to receive the baby.

Our first thoughts went to the building of a pine plank cabin; but after we'd considered the cost of lumber and the even greater expense of getting it hauled to us, we gave up the idea and looked about us for new ones. The homes of most of our neighbors were built of materials that existed right here on the land—native stone, adobe bricks, and cottonwood poles for rafters. And, after studying such dwellings awhile, we found that we were better pleased with them than we'd be with any sort of lumber house that we could afford to build with our limited means.

At last, we decided on adobe blocks. I didn't know how to make them, but my "renter" Cleofas Natividad did. And this might prove a way to collect my rent.

I went to talk with Cleofas. He couldn't understand English and I couldn't understand Spanish; but with lots of gesturing and pointing and explaining, we finally got together on the trade. For ten dollars in labor, Cleofas agreed to make me one thousand adobe bricks twelve by four by eighteen inches. For ten dollars more, he was to transport them from where he made them at his well to the house site Bessie and I had chosen.

Cleofas, with the help of his many children, set to work. He made the bricks out of a mixture of mud, grass, and goat manure. The children did the mixing with their bare feet, trampling the ingredients as Cleofas put them into a hole he'd dug into the ground.

Once the mud was of the proper consistency, it was scooped out, put into wooden molds, then laid out on the bare ground to dry. When the bricks were finally "cured," Cleofas caught up his six burros, loaded six bricks to each burro, then drove them over the rough hills to unload and stack the bricks on a high point above the hot spring.

Bessie and I had chosen this spot with care. It was high, with everything open to the south, so that we had a wonderful view of the Rio Grande canyon below, and would catch every breeze that came across the mountains in Mexico during the summer. Yet we were still far enough down the slope so that in the wintertime we'd be protected from any wild winds that came from the north.

Since working on our new house would require several trips a day, up and down the steep, half-mile slope from our camp to the house site, we decided to move camp to the new site before starting work. We got Cleofas and his burros to help us again.

But after we'd erected our tents and thought we had everything set for going to work, it finally came to us that we'd made one rather serious miscalculation. Our hot spring was close now, just under the hill, in fact; but packing water for mortar-making up a slope that was almost a sheer drop for about one hundred and fifty feet was going to require a stupendous amount of back-breaking labor.

This set me to thinking. There just had to be some easier way to get water up that slope.

At first, the only thing I could think of was to improve the zig-zag trail leading down to water. This I did by picking out rocks and building shelves to hold dirt, and exaggerating the zigs and zags to make the climb gentler. But that incline stood at something like a seventy-five to eighty degree angle, so that, no matter what I did to the trail, it was still a breath-taking struggle for a man to climb it with a couple of buckets of water.

Finally, I came up with a solution and a good one. I stretched a heavy steel wire from a steel pin wedged into a rock fissure at camp down to another at the spring. Once pulled tight, the wire stood at something like a forty-five degree angle and was clear of all pro-truding ledges. Then, at the top, I built a windlass, around which I wrapped a strong fishing cord. The loose end of the line was tied to a window-sash pulley on the wire, and to this a harness snap was fastened to hold a bucket bail. The weight of the empty bucket, descending on my wire, was sufficient to turn the windlass; and down at the bottom, I erected a bumper to stop the bucket where it would fill. Once the bucket was full of water, I could draw it back up the wire cable by winding the windlass. By testing and making a few adjustments, I soon had our "slow-drawlic" water system operating so easily that a five-year-old child could have drawn water from the spring.

Now, with everything ready, Cleofas and I began actual con-struction of the house. That was in September. Cleofas was a faith-ful worker, and he took pride in helping us. Together, we worked from early morning each day till sunset, mixing mortar and laying bricks.

For door sills, I used long flat stones that Cleofas dragged from the surrounding hills with his ever-faithful burros. Such stones were also used for headers above the doors and windows and to frame the fireplace. We wrecked an abandoned hut a mile up the valley and dragged off such timbers as we could use. One long straight log we used as a center pole. There were some smaller poles, too, which we used as rafters. We cut cane from along the river with which to roof the rafters, tying the cane down hard and fast with strings of split yucca blades. Then over the cane we heaped a six-inch layer of damp clay, which dried and hardened to make a good water-proof roof and later did much to keep our house cool in the summer.

By using all we could of available material, we cut down on material I had to order from Marathon. All in all, the nails, hinges, small amount of lumber, and one window I did have to order came to only around ten dollars. And since Cleofas' work was credited toward the lease money he owed me, that ten dollars was my total cash outlay for a good, weather-proof, one-room cabin, twelve by fourteen feet and nine feet high.

We finished our work three or four days before the baby came; but for all our hurrying, the child was still not born in the cabin. The mortar wouldn't dry; and since the weather was cool now, we didn't think it would be wise to move Bessie into a cool, damp cabin at such a time.

Cleofas and I tried to hurry the drying process by building up a roaring fire in the fireplace and keeping it going day and night. But it was a waste of precious wood. It just didn't seem to matter how hot we kept the room, the mortar still took its own time about drying.

The fire was still going and the cabin was still damp about sundown of November 28 when Bessie called me. The time was here, she told me.

This was the one time of all our venture that I had dreaded

most. Now, if I had made a mistake in bringing my family out here away from civilization, Bessie would pay for it. This was the one terrifying risk I had taken.

I rushed down to Cleofas' dugout to get him and his wife. *Señora* Natividad came back with me to the house, and Cleofas got on his burro to ride downriver the six miles to Boquillas, Mexico, to get a doctor who was employed there by a silver mining company.

When *Señora* Natividad and I got back to the house, we assured Bessie that Cleofas would bring the doctor; but Bessie just shook her head.

"I think maybe you'd better re-read Dr. Lynch's instructions," she told me.

And while we at the house were waiting, Cleofas was making the ride of his life. By now it was pitch dark; and with the coming of darkness, the urgency of the trip seemed greater to Cleofas. He whipped his burro with a quirt. He hammered its flanks with his heels. He swore his mightiest oaths. But of course, the only real exertion made on that trip was by Cleofas; the burro traveled at his usual gait.

Exhausted, Cleofas finally reached the mining camp. And there he learned bad news. The doctor was gone, visiting a sick Mexican about twelve miles away.

There was nothing for Cleofas to do but turn around and come back to bring us the bad news.

But in the meantime, Lucille, our second daughter, had come into the world. It had been an easy birth, due, we felt, to the baths Bessie had taken in the spring and to the vigorous climb up and down the slope from the spring to the campsite.

When it was over, I was so grateful I nearly wept. Bessie had come through the ordeal wonderfully well, and the baby was strong and healthy looking.

I had acted as doctor, carefully following Dr. Lynch's instructions; and Cleofas' wife had acted as midwife. The two of us, using the prescribed medicines and our one surgical instrument— a thoroughly scalded pair of scissors—did such a satisfactory job of delivering the baby that by the time Cleofas returned, we had everything under control and were able to help quiet and comfort him after his arduous ride.

By morning, all three patients were much improved, Cleofas so much so that he agreed to ride fifteen miles up into the foothills of the Chisos Mountains to bring back Mrs. John Rice, who had been one of our visitors at the spring awhile back. She had offered to come and stay with us a week or so when the baby came.

Within the next three or four days, the house dried out, and Mrs. Rice and I started moving the furniture into it.

Bessie and I had brought with us from Midland two iron bedsteads with coil springs and mattresses. After we'd moved these into the cabin, along with one rocking chair, four split-bottom straight chairs, an extra large oak dining table, an antique walnut chest, a goods-box wardrobe, and a Hoover kitchen cabinet, Mrs. Rice and I had used up all the room space. There was no place left for the cookstove.

So, following Mrs. Rice's suggestion, I devised a potrack in the fireplace to hold vessels for boiling purposes. A dutch oven served for baking bread, pies, and cakes; and a skillet and a frying pan could be placed directly over the coals.

When finally we were moved inside, we found it a rather tight fit, to say the least. But it was snug and warm for the winter that was coming on.

And nobody with a new house and a new baby has anything to complain about.

Twelve

ONCE THE HOUSE WAS UP and we had moved in, my next job was to haul up enough wood to last through the short winter.

Up the Rio Grande, something like a mile away, there was an unlimited supply of good mesquite wood. But how to get it home?

I could have hired Cleofas again, of course. But then, I'd already used up the rent labor he owed me. Also, what with helping me build the house, Cleofas had spent so much time working for me that he needed to get back to his own work. So I decided to buy a burro of my own.

After inquiring around and looking at this burro and that, I finally found what I wanted at the pens of Ventura Bustas, who lived up the Rio Grande at the little village of San Vicente.

He was a big mouse-colored burro with gray sides and belly and a streak of brown down his backbone. I paid twelve dollars for him and a saddle, and undertook to ride him home. But he traveled so slowly under me that I finally lost patience and got off and walked. I named him Boomer, but I don't think I ever fooled him into trying to live up to the vigorous sound of his name.

I brought Boomer home one day and turned him loose to graze in the lush grass around our cabin and then the next day had to walk back to San Vicente, where there was hardly any grass at all, and bring him home again. That evening when I turned him loose, I put hobbles on him. The next morning's search for him wound up along in the afternoon at the same place—San Vicente. After that, I kept him staked on a long rope, sometimes on the grass around the cabin, other times down in the cane brakes along the Rio Grande.

In spite of all this trouble, Boomer proved to be a gentle and faithful worker. That is, he was gentle for me to handle. But he loathed chickens and was never very gentle in his treatment of them. The same day I'd bought him, I'd also traded for a dozen hens and a rooster of the gay-colored Mexican chickens. Any time I fed grain to Boomer, these chickens would try to rob his feed box. Boomer would get so angry that I was almost afraid to approach him. He'd kick at the chickens. He'd try to paw them. He'd bare his teeth and chase them all over the place. And then, if by some miracle, he managed to get them all run off at once, he'd lay back his ears and bray at them, just daring one to come back and try to get any more of his feed.

Boomer stayed right with me, though, when it came to packing in my winter wood. Sometimes I'd tie two or three poles on each side of his saddle, but never did I have him decide that he was overloaded and balk on me. I'd get him loaded, pick up the lead rope, and say, "All right, let's go, Boomer." And he'd grunt and give his tail a wring or two and keep right up with me over the steepest and roughest sort of trails.

Lovie was crazy about Boomer and rode him more than anybody else did. Sometimes when she was riding him up or down the steep banks to the river, or along the brink of some precipice, I'd get scared that the burro might make a false step and fall with her. But only once in all the time I owned him did he lose his footing.

That was on a washday, when we were all coming up the steep trail from the pools of the Tornillo.

We'd thought when we first moved up into the new cabin that we could draw hot water right up from the spring and wash with it without ever having to heat the water. But that was one plan that didn't work. The water, though hot enough, was too hard. Soap wouldn't dissolve in it, and neither would grease and dirt. On account of this, we usually took off from work about once a week and hauled our washing down to the softer water in the Tornillo. And it always fell Boomer's lot to carry the paraphernalia to and from the creek, generally with Lovie riding on top.

On this particular day, the washing was done and the clothes spread out on the thorny bushes to dry and bleach in the hot sun. We'd started back to the house, with me leading Boomer and Lovie riding him, and Bessie following behind with the baby.

We were about halfway up the slant, rounding a sharp bend of a ledge where the trail was barely wide enough for Boomer's hoofs. Behind me, I could tell by the way Boomer had slowed his walk that he was feeling out the ground with each foot before trusting his weight to it.

Then something happened. I never knew quite what. I heard a wild scramble of hoofs. Bessie screamed, and I wheeled to find Boomer half off the ledge and fighting for a foothold.

Barely in time, I grabbed Lovie from his back, then almost fell with her myself, thrown off balance by the shotgun I carried in my other hand.

Tubs, buckets and washboard spilled from Boomer's back, to go clattering and banging down the shaley slant into the deep-cut *arroyo* below. But Boomer didn't follow them. He still had both forefeet hooked over that shelf of rock and he kept that hold, hanging there like a cat. Then, carefully, grunting and straining, he pawed for purchase with his hind feet, got it, and settled himself back on the ledge at last, lying flat on his belly, with every foot set and braced. Here he rested for awhile, looking up at us, while we looked down at him.

Then, finally, with a sigh and a grunt, the burro started getting his feet under him, one foot at a time, and taking it slow, till he was up and waiting for me to collect the plunder and load him once more.

When I sold Boomer several years later to a Mexican who lived some ten miles south of the Rio Grande, I forgot to tell the man to keep the burro tied. So it was but a few days later that he showed up at the pens of Ventura Bustas, wearing a pair of hobbles and looking mighty proud to be at home again.

Nobody could ever quite figure out how Boomer managed to swim the Rio Grande with hobbles on.

Thirteen

THAT FIRST WINTER was one of financial worry for me. We'd collected something like one hundred and fifty dollars from bathers at the spring. I'd earned a little more by buying baled chinograss from the Mexicans and reselling it to fishermen and bathers. Also, I'd learned to braid quirts and cow whips and had picked up a few dollars selling them to cowmen.

But our living expenses had eaten into my small capital pretty heavily. Christmas was coming on, and there was little chance for any more income from bathers before spring.

So I turned to fur-trapping. I set about a dozen steel traps along the game trails and baited them with birds and rabbits. I visited the traps once a day to pick up what animals I'd caught. Tex ran the trapline with me and could never understand why I wouldn't let her tear the animals apart. I caught beavers, foxes, opossums, skunks. The skunks were the most numerous; but to skin one of these little animals without clouding myself in a fog of strong scent, I found impossible. Cleofas showed me how to set fire to cotton rags and stand in the smoke to get rid of some of the smell, but sometimes I thought the scent of the burning cotton was almost as bad as the skunk.

I caught some huge coons there along the Rio Grande, and all with the blackest fur I'd ever seen on that animal.

During the daytime, when I wasn't busy skinning and stretching my pelts, I hunted duck quite a bit, fished some, and started cutting and dragging up poles and river cane to the house. With these I began construction of arbors against the house to help break the fierce heat of the sun for the next summer.

We had a good Christmas that year. A few weeks beforehand, Lovie put in her request for the one present she must have. She wanted a cat.

Finally, Bessie consented. "All right, Lovie," she said. "I'll speak to Santa Claus about bringing you a toy cat."

"But Lovie doesn't want a stuffed cat," Lovie wailed. "Lovie wants a raw cat!"

For our tree, I selected an evergreen native to the region—the guayacán, which nature seemed already to have decorated for the purpose. Its tiny leaves were waxy green, and all up and down every branch were pods enclosing bright and orange-red seeds, an excellent substitute for holly. With a huge fire in the fireplace, a few simple presents from one of the mail order houses, and a "raw" cat for Lovie, ours was as good a Christmas as we'd ever had.

We made a holiday of it and visited a newly-married couple who had come to homestead a piece of land near San Vicente. They had set up housekeeping in a dugout and were proud of the start they were making.

They went to considerable trouble to have a good meal for our visit, and what happened to it must have been a humiliating thing for the bride. We'd just sat down to the table when a wise old

Plymouth Rock hen walked into the room on her way to a nest in the corner. Confused by our presence in her pathway, she selected the most direct route, hopped up onto the table, and walked calmly across a big cake and two egg custards, leaving deep footprints in each.

The bride gasped at the sight, then almost wept.

Bessie tried to console the girl. She took a spoon and dipped out the hen-tracks, and we all assured the bride that her food was as good as before, and went to work to prove it.

But although we ate heartily, I don't think the poor girl ever again looked on homesteading in quite the same happy light as she had before.

Early that spring I made a trip to Marathon to sell my furs and to buy a supply of provisions. I went with Jesse Deemer, who lived four miles down the river from me. Jesse had a pair of wild Spanish mules, but no buggy. I had a buckboard, but no mules. So we went into partnership for the trip to town.

Bessie and the two children rode with us as far as the Rice home, where they were to visit till we returned.

Jesse's mules, skittish as they were, gave us no real trouble until we were within about twelve miles of Marathon. Then a little scrap of white paper blew across the road ahead of them. The paper might as well have been a grizzly bear. The little mules, fat and nervous as rabbits, snorted, reared up on their hind feet, then lit out, each trying to go in a different direction.

Deemer and I did our best, but luck was against us. The buckboard struck a boulder, pitched Deemer and me out, then skidded on its side till the mules finally straddled a yucca plant strong enough to stop them.

We were a sorry looking lot when we finally crippled in to Marathon late that afternoon to inquire of a blacksmith who might repair our buckboard.

In spite of the fact that my furs had been dragged and rolled in the dust during the runaway, I had the good fortune to meet a man from San Antonio who was willing to pay me a premium price to get them so he could have them made up for his bride.

Even at that, by the time I'd paid the blacksmith for repairing a broken tongue, a sprung dashboard, and a battered top to the buckboard, I barely had money enough left to buy my groceries.

Then on the way back home, Deemer's mules spooked at the sight of a sack of corn that had evidently slipped from some freighter's wagon. They took off for a second run.

However, while Deemer and I couldn't hold the runaways, we did manage to keep them away from obstructions that might wreck my buckboard again. And when they finally ran themselves down, we circled back and picked up the sack of corn. This we later divided between my chickens and Deemer's mules, although for the life of me, I never could really feel that the mules deserved any of it.

For the next several weeks, I was pretty worried. I didn't have enough money to make my land payment when it came due in May. There was nobody to borrow it from and apparently no way to make it. It was too late in the season to trap more furs and too early for the bathers to start coming in. Yet I felt more than ever that I must hang onto our new home. The hot spring and our leisurely way of living had definitely improved my health. And all of us liked the new life we had entered into.

I was beginning to get really desperate when one day a man named Rutledge paid me a visit. He was J. W. Rutledge, a customs officer at Boquillas, and he wanted to buy the section of my land that lay near the custom house. He said he'd been meaning to buy it for some time before I had, and had finally sent in his bid on it right after my bid had been accepted in Austin. Rutledge offered me seven hundred and fifty dollars for the section.

To me, it was a godsend. Up to now, I had found no profitable use for so much land, and I certainly needed the money.

"But I thought I had to prove up on the land before I could sell it," I told Rutledge.

"No," he told me. "You can sell it after you've lived on it for one year."

That being the case, I agreed to sell Rutledge the section, provided he advance me enough to make my second-year payment on the rest of the property.

And now, with the extra money, I could start work on a bath house that I had had in mind for some time. With a good private bath house and more accommodations, I figured I could draw more guests and ask more for the baths.

I was even able, with Rutledge's money, to lease Gordon's spring when he finally wrote and asked thirty dollars a year for it.

Fourteen

HERMAN JACOBS, who had homesteaded eight sections of land above the McKinney Hills, laid the stone for my bath house. Herman was a big, strong German about twenty-five years old, who had served an apprenticeship as a stonemason in Germany before he'd left his home country and come to Texas. He was the fastest and best worker of native stone that I ever saw.

With the help of several Mexicans that I hired at a dollar a day, I'd selected loose stones that had fallen from the nearby cliffs. We'd carried them to the building site ahead of time.

Then, in March, Herman came and started laying them. I laid out to Herman my plans for the bath house, answered a few pertinent questions, then turned the heavy work over to him. And he knew what to do with it, too. The first swipe I saw him make with a mortar trowel assured me that he was going to be worth every cent of the four dollars a day that I'd agreed to pay him.

I had one Mexican still gathering rocks. Herman put another

to washing and scrubbing the rocks we'd gathered with a steel brush, the third to mixing mortar, and the fourth to waiting on him, bringing him rocks and mortar as he needed them.

Part of the time I helped, too; but even then, all of us put together couldn't keep Herman in mud and rocks as fast as he called for them. He could take one glance at a pile of say a hundred rocks, point, and say: "Bring me that one." And nine times out of ten that rock fit exactly the place he had in mind for it. If not, one or two quick strokes with his stone hammer made it fit.

Herman worked and sweated and worried at a furious pace. He worked that way because that was the way he'd been taught to work. He sweated because of his exertions and because of the heat. But his worries were a different matter.

Herman Jacobs' worries had to do with Kaiser Wilhelm back in Germany.

"Building war machines, they are," Herman would rage. "Europe, they would conquer. The whole world! The fools! The *dumkopfs!* Start a slaughterhouse, they will! Biggest slaughter the world ever know!"

Eventually, he revealed that he was an officer in the reserve of the Kaiser's army. It was for this reason that he had left his homeland and come to this strange country. He wanted no part of the Kaiser's war machine. Herman predicted for us, that spring of 1910, that the war would start in 1914, and that he would be recalled to serve.

But in those days, Germany seemed far away, and we didn't pay too much attention to Herman. We just figured him for a big, gloomy, hard-working German and let it go at that.

We built the bath house twenty feet by twenty, making three feet thick the wall that would have to bear the brunt of the floods when the Rio Grande got up. The other walls we built twenty inches thick.

We capped the spring and led the water through rock channels to the various tubs, which were built of rock and plastered over with cement. At each tub, we cemented in two-inch gate valves that could be opened and shut, then arranged a drain hole in the bottom of each tub that could be plugged, thereby raising the water to the top of the tub before letting it out through an upper drain.

For roofing, we used one-by-eight lumber over two-by-six rafters, set at such a slant that when the Rio Grande flooded, the weight of the water tended to hold the roof down, rather than lifting and washing it away.

While we were still working on the bath house, Lucille, our chunky baby, began to crawl. And one morning, without my knowing it, she followed behind me when I went out of the cabin to my windlass to draw up a bucket of water.

The first I knew of her presence was when I heard her cry out and saw her tumble off the ledge beside me.

Instantly, I dropped the windlass, letting the halfdrawn bucket go slamming back to the bottom. I leaped down the slope after her, slipping and sliding as I went.

There were only about thirty feet of this precipitous slope before it broke away to a sheer drop of fifty feet. If I couldn't catch the baby before she reached that precipice, she couldn't possibly escape death.

I screamed at the bath house workmen, telling them to catch the baby, but didn't know whether or not they heard me. I threw myself down the slant with all the speed I could and knew the sickening horror of being too late.

Then, just at the brink, one of the thorny branches of an ocotillo seemed to reach out and catch the baby's dress.

There Lucille hung, already half over the edge of the precipice, until I could get down and get my hands on her. And just below, I saw Herman and all the Mexicans lined up, their arms lifted to catch her.

Our trail that led from the house down to the spring went past that particular ocotillo plant, and a dozen times its thorns had pricked me and just as many times, I'd sworn to grub it up. But I'd never got around to it. And after that, I never did. It wasn't too long, either, before I built a fence to keep the children from falling off that ledge.

Before Jacobs and the other workers and I were finished with the bath house that spring, bathers began coming in. Many of them shook their heads when they saw that every time the Rio Grande overflowed, the house would be under water. It'd never stand, they all predicted. Jesse Deemer said it wouldn't.

But Charlie Hess, an experienced mining man, came by one day, studied it for a moment, and said emphatically: "Langford, that house'll be standing there when the trumpet sounds."

Hess may have been exaggerating some, but that bath house has withstood every flood that's come its way up to now, and there've been several.

When the work was done, I paid Herman Jacobs and he went back to his homestead. Soon after he'd proved up on his land, he moved to Oklahoma. We later learned that Herman married in Oklahoma and that he and his wife had had two children.

It was several years later before we heard of Herman again. By that time, as he had predicted, Germany was deep in a war, and Herman had got his order to report back for duty in the German army. And our big, gloomy, hard-working Herman had taken his pistol, shot his wife and both children, then blown out his own brains. The great slaughter that Herman Jacobs had predicted was on.

Fifteen

AT VARIOUS TIMES, some very interesting people came to the spring to visit. Occasionally, a visitor would stop over on his way to or from riding the rapids of the Rio Grande through the canyons of Santa Helena, Mariscal, Reagan, and Boquillas. This is wild, dangerous country, with the cliffs standing so high and sharply over the water that in many places the sunlight never reaches it. Several men have been smashed against the canyon walls by the roaring waters and killed in their attempt to ride their boats through.

But this did not stop men like Henry B. du Pont, of the famous du Pont family, or Colonel Martin Crimmins and his photographer friend, Lieutenant Commander Claude Young. The fascination of the unknown kept these men coming back to chart the unexplored and to record in pictures the wild beauty of the region, inaccessible to men less determined and less interested in the strange manifestations of nature.

Others came to the spring only to bathe and relax and take their vacations. About the most vigorous relaxers I ever saw were the two Marathon cowhands who came that first summer and for many summers afterward. They camped near the spring, bathed, fished, drank tequila and sotol, and fought each other. Every day they fought, all up and down the river, and apparently just for the hell of it, for they seemed to be the best of friends.

They'd come and pitch camp and set out their fish lines, and then it wouldn't be any time before they'd be squared off and having themselves the most uproarious fist fight you could imagine. From a quarter mile away, up or down the river you could hear one of them swearing at the other, sneering at him, telling him, "Why, you so-and-so, you pulled that last punch! You didn't put all you had into it. Now get up and fight like a man. Hit me! Right here on the jaw. And you'd better hit me hard. Because if you don't, I'm going to hang one on you that'll show you what I'm talking about."

When they were at their best, they sounded like two young bulls fighting. Sometimes, I'd go stand on the cliff above and watch as they laughed and swore and fought each other till one of them finally went down in the rocks and was unable to get up again.

Then the other one would go get the tequila and sotol for both of them, and they'd sit and drink and laugh at the fight they'd just had and finally, after the beaten man had got back sufficient strength, they'd go off together and take a hot bath or maybe go take a catfish off their lines.

Once in awhile, they'd bring some other cowhands along with them. I remember the day one of the boys, grouchy drunk, kept grumbling about the cooking. The others, finally tiring of his grumbling, picked him up, carried him out of the shade of the camp, and tied him to a yucca plant out in the broiling sun. They left him there for something like half a day to think over his last disparaging remarks about camp food.

But more often, the original two cowhands came alone, without the others. They seemed to have their best times when there were just the two of them to relax together.

We had one strange visitor who for years came periodically to the spring. He was a bachelor named George Lewis, and he owned a farm somewhere in East Texas. George claimed that he walked every one of the hundreds of miles from his farm to the Big Bend. I couldn't swear to that, but anyone in the Big Bend country could testify that George certainly walked the eighty-five miles from Marathon to the Rio Grande. He refused to ride with anyone. He accepted few favors, and ate with no one. He was cheerful enough, and humorous, always laughing and talking—about anything and everything but himself.

On his trips, George carried only the barest essentials. A few extra pieces of clothing, a blanket, sometimes a few cans of sardines and a box of crackers. He'd come down, take a few baths, then one day shoulder his pack. "Well, goodby," he'd tell me. "I'm on my way."

On one particularly hot day when he was leaving, I filled a quart canteen for him and insisted that he take it along.

"It's twelve miles to the first water hole," I warned him.

He just grinned at me. "I know," he said. "And who'd want to pack a load of water that far in hot weather like this?" And George Lewis was gone.

Sometimes domestic troubles were brought right into camp by the guests. I remember a chiropractor and his wife who pulled in late one afternoon, loaded down with camping equipment and chiropractic implements. It was apparent from the start that the wife wasn't happy about coming into this wild and rugged country. But she went ahead and started their supper while the doctor discussed arrangements with me to open up an office for treating patients. By full dark, we still hadn't come to an agreement, and the doctor's wife began calling him to supper. He ignored her and went on talking to me.

After about the fifth time to call the doctor, his wife came after him. She called him out of my house, hit him over the head with a lighted lantern, and let loose with a barrage of abuse that must have seared his ears.

And that couple didn't even wait till daylight to pack up and start moving back to more civilized country.

Out of all the guests who came for the baths, it was only natural that a few of them would be cranks. There were some who would select a certain tub to bathe in, with the firm conviction that the water flowing into that particular tub was hotter than that in the other tubs.

Most people loved the solitude of the country, but there were a few who reacted adversely to it. There was one boy from Houston who couldn't get off to sleep without the usual noise of a city. He persuaded a couple of other boys in the camp to beat on pans and tin cans near him until he could get off to sleep every night.

But just about the most cantankerous visitor we had was an old man I'll call Coffee because that isn't his name.

Coffee arrived from Fort Stockton some hundred and fifty miles away, driving a pair of sleepy burros hitched to a light buckboard. Riding beside him on the seat was a mongrel dog he called Chum.

Coffee pitched camp in a nook of the cliff wall in the shade of some mesquites. Before he even bothered to unhitch and hobble out his burros, he built up a campfire and put on a pot of coffee. I happened along the river trail just as he was pouring his first cup, and stopped to get acquainted. Convention demanded that he offer me a cup, and he did, but with obvious reluctance.

He was a tall old man, maybe sixty-five, and evidently pretty soured out with the world. Under question, he admitted that he was sick and wanted to take some baths; but just what his ailment was, he never revealed. Coffee was not a talkative man.

He paid in advance the dime for one bath, took it that first day. Thereafter, he just squatted on his heels by the campfire, boiling coffee and drinking it and smoking a foul-smelling pipe, and staring out across the Rio Grande. He didn't hunt, didn't fish, hardly ate anything. Sometimes he'd cook up a little food, but the dog Chum got most of that, along with a lot of bitter, sarcastic comments on how sorry and no-account he was.

After three or four days, I noticed that Coffee wasn't taking his baths. I came to the conclusion that the old man was broke and couldn't pay for more. I went down one morning and talked to him.

"Look, Mr. Coffee," I said. "You're sick, and you've come a long way. If you're short of money, we'll just forget it. You go ahead and take your baths. You can send me the money later if you want to."

The old man still squatted on his heels, puffing at his pipe and staring at me as if he couldn't quite believe he'd heard what I'd said. Then suddenly he shot to his feet, his fierce old eyes hot with anger. In a scathing voice and in no uncertain terms, he informed me that he wasn't in the habit of accepting charity, that for my information, he had plenty of money to pay his way wherever he went and always had had money and always would. Furthermore, he went on, he'd taken a bath and it had cured him, so why in the hell should he keep on bathing every day?

I couldn't answer that one. I left his camp as quickly as possible, feeling as cheap and cowed as his dog Chum looked every time the old man lashed out at him.

Coffee spent nearly three weeks squatting there on his heels in the shade of the mesquites, smoking his pipe and drinking the bitter scalding coffee that he kept brewing on top of the old grounds from the last brewing.

Then finally, one morning, he hitched up his burros, called Chum up into the springseat beside him, and left out.

So far as I know, he left "cured," but cured of what I never learned. Certainly, he wasn't cured of coffee-drinking or pipe-smoking, or of his cantankerous nature. For as his wagon rattled over the rocks up Tornillo Canyon, I could hear his coffee pot rattling around loose in the bed of his wagon; I could see clouds of smoke fogging out of his old pipe. And the last I heard of him as he drove out of sight, he was berating Chum for sitting so close to him in the springseat.

Sixteen

THAT YEAR, the spring rains failed to come. Light showers fell in March. April was dry, and by May, a hot blazing sun had parched and withered the few plants that had sprouted in the fields and gardens. Without the intervention of the gods, there'd be hunger among my neighbors along the Rio Grande before the year was out.

So the gods were called on. Prayers were prayed and homage paid to the old gods who'd been in command along the Rio Grande long before the first European set foot on the shores of the New World. And then, just to play it safe, honor was also paid to the God of the Christians.

Nightly for two weeks, prayers were held in every dugout and *jacal*. For the same length of time, no man drank alcoholic beverages. And day after day, the *jefe*, or chief, of each village called his people together and led them from one barren field to the next, where they knelt in the dust and prayed.

I learned that the final ceremony this year was to be held at San Vicente on the Mexican side of the river, and persuaded Bessie to attend it with me.

When that day came, we mounted Lovie on Boomer, Bessie carried Lucille on the horse, and I led Boomer, walking the five miles of river trail to the upper crossing, not far from the old San Vicente fort.

A cheerful little boy, Francisco Padilla, awaited us there with horses. We forded the river, then rode up through a deep cut in the dirt bank. We passed through a tall stand of river cane.

Just as we came out into the open patches of cultivated ground, we were startled by the sound of six pistol shots fired in rapid succession. We looked to our right. There, the village *jefe,* with a smoking revolver in his hand, was rising from his knees in the middle of a dusty field. About him, the villagers, who had been bowed in prayer, rose to their feet, too.

Now, the *jefe* led the way across the sun-scorched fields toward a little cone-shaped hill with a huge wooden cross standing in the top of it.

"La Loma de la Santa Cruz," Francisco explained to us. The Hill of the Sainted Cross.

Walking directly behind the *jefe,* two men carried between them a box resting on two short sticks. This, I'd been told, was the *nicho,* a box containing the image of Christ, lavishly decorated with artificial flowers. Behind the *nicho,* came the rest of the villagers.

We swung our horses about and trailed after the procession.

A huge, white-breasted hawk perched on the cross, watched warily as the people approached, and finally flew away in alarm.

At the foot of the hill, the *jefe* stood aside. The two men carrying the *nicho* struggled on up the steep incline and deposited the box at the foot of the cross and knelt beside it. Then the *jefe* lifted his reloaded revolver and fired it into the air. Instantly, the worshippers dropped to the ground. On hands and knees they climbed

Boquillas Canyon, Carmen Mountains in background

The Rio Grande

Carmen Mountains, recumbent Indian chief on horizon

J. O. Langford, Bessie, Lovie, and Lucille

Aerial view of Santa Elena Canyon

Aerial view of Carmen Mountains

Santa Elena Canyon from a distance

Entrance to Green Gulch

Ruins at Glen Springs

Lovie and Tex

The Window

The Langfords' first home at Hot Springs

The bath house

The Rain Ceremony

El viejo

Rio Grande, Sentinel Peak in background

Carmen Mountains, showing Shot Tower

An airial view of Marietal Canyon

Pummel Peak from the east, *ocotillo* and *lechuguilla* in foreground

Slaughter Cave in Santa Elena Canyon

Along the Rio Grande in Boquillas Canyon

Pulliam Ridge from Green Gulch, with Century Plant in foreground

the hill, while the *jefe* fired his pistol several more times at regular intervals.

We waited at the bottom of the hill. Above us, the people gathered around the cross and the *nicho*. There, on their knees, they prayed again, their voices rising and falling in unison as they called on Jesus Christ and the old Indian gods to bless their fields with rain.

At the conclusion of their ceremony, they rose, quietly followed the *jefe* and the two men carrying the *nicho* down the hill and out across the fields to a tree. There, after more prayers and six more shots from the *jefe's* pistol, the *nicho* was placed in the forks of the tree, where it was to remain, Francisco explained, until the rain started falling. Then the men would hasten to bring it to the home of the *jefe*.

Now that the praying was done, the *jefe* came to receive Bessie and me and make us welcome at his home. Food was brought to the tables under the arbor—*frijoles, tortillas, fritada* (a blood pudding), *cabrito* (roast kid goat), and coffee. We ate, savoring the highly seasoned food, then sat back to wait for the final ritual.

This was colorful pageantry, based on a story so old that no one seems to know its origin or its exact significance.

It started that afternoon with the music of a string band, followed by a dance around the *nicho*, which had been moved temporarily to a table under the arbor. All the Mexicans participated in the dance, but only the principal actors of the pageant were in costume.

Francisco pointed them out for us. First, there was *El Monarco*, the man who ranks above all others. Then *El Capitán* and *La Capitana*, the man and woman; and *La Malinche*, the girl. And, finally, there was *El Viejo*, the old one. All but *El Viejo* were dressed in bright red costumes (*trajes*) and wore headgear (*montera*) decorated with small mirrors, pieces of bright tin, turkey feathers, rope fiber and horsehair tinted red, and small shells. The costumes were long tunic affairs, with a fringe around the bottom. The fringe was made by forming a knot in the end of a cord some six inches long, which was passed through a hole in a piece of bright tin about half an inch square, then through a four-inch length of cane. The bright metal, striking against the cane, made tinkling musical sounds as the actors moved about.

Each dancer carried in his left hand a bow and arrow (*arco* and *flecha*) decorated with pieces of red tin and splotched with red stain, representing blood. In the other hand he carried a *guaje*, or gourd rattle, which was adorned with paper and contained a few pebbles.

El Viejo was dressed as hideously as possible, wearing a false face with a frightful leer and a headgear with big mule ears. From the back of his headgear hung a queue made of gray fiber that dragged the ground. Like the others, *El Viejo* carried a gourd rattle in one hand, but in the other hand he grasped a long braided rawhide whip which he occasionally cracked over his head with a report equal to that of the *jefe's* pistol.

Sided by *El Capitán*, *La Capitana* approached the *nicho*, where she bowed and snapped an empty bow four times. This was the signal for the ceremony to begin. Then *La Capitana* moved along, making room for others who came, two by two, to imitate her performance.

Gradually, a circle was formed, and the dance began, a prancy step accompanied by the measured rattling of the *guajes*. *El Monarco's* voice lifted in high whoops. *El Viejo* cracked his whip over his head. Dust rose from under scores of moccasined feet, thudding in unison. Before long, the very earth seemed to shake with the same mad rhythm.

Occasionally, *La Capitana* gave a signal and all the dancers stopped to rest on the benches under the arbors. They sat and visited and smoked until *La Capitana* gave the signal for them to start dancing again.

It was a weird sight, but a fascinating one. It held us gripped there, so that we lost all sense of time and were conscious only of sight, sound, and movement.

At last, however, *El Viejo* left the ring, only to return a moment later and reveal his true and hateful nature. Riding a burro now, he broke into the ring, grasped the virgin *Malinche* and tried to ride away with her to the mountains.

But *El Monarco* was watching for him. With a cry of outrage, he raised his bow and "shot" *El Viejo* from his burro.

The Old One fell to the ground and lay there, and the others danced by and knelt to "drink of his blood," and to make motions of smearing it on their clothes and on their bows and arrows, and then went dancing on again.

Three more times they danced past the vanquished *El Viejo*. The first time was to place their bows upon his body, the second to leave their arrows there; and finally, concluding the dance, to discard their gourd rattles upon the corpse of *El Viejo*.

It was after night when Bessie and I led Boomer and the sleeping children up to our cabin above the hot spring. I glanced once at the sky as we went inside to get ready for bed and saw not one trace of a cloud among the stars. Yet when daylight came, rain was pouring down, and it continued to pour. By noon, every *arroyo* was alive with water and by night the Rio Grande had risen four feet. The rain soaked the parched brown fields. Eagerly the people planted their corn, pumpkin seeds, and grain. Ten days later, the planting over, the rains fell again for four consecutive days. The river rose ten feet. A bountiful harvest was assured.

Evidently the gods had been pleased.

Seventeen

ONE OF MY BIG WORRIES when we first moved into the Big Bend country was whether or not Bessie could stand the loneliness. Everyone I had talked to in Alpine had said essentially the same thing—nobody could stand the isolation of such a place. The German homesteader had moved off before he proved up on the land because of it. The county surveyor hadn't been able to persuade his wife to move onto the spring because of it. The Fort Stockton man who wanted the spring still didn't want it badly enough to hold out against the loneliness of living here to prove up on it. And Mr. Landrum at La Noria told me that at least one white settler woman he knew had finally become completely deranged from the sheer loneliness of this vast country.

But I need not have worried about Bessie. For one thing, we had the visitors to the spring. I'm sure if it hadn't been for them, we'd both have suffered a good deal. But they came, and we were as glad to see them as we were to have the added income they brought us. Often, to make them feel welcome, Bessie would cook up special dishes and send the food down by Lovie.

One day a number of people drove down to the camp grounds just before noon. Bessie had a pan full of hot rolls in the oven, and when they were done, she put some in a basket and called Lovie.

Lovie came to the kitchen from the next room, her panties hanging jauntily from one finger. In the hot weather, she had got into the habit of taking off the binding little undergarments.

"Lovie," Bessie told her, "put your panties on and run down and take these hot rolls to the new visitors."

Lovie was getting a little tired of running these errands. "Well, look, Mother," she said. "Why don't you go? You've already got your panties on."

But aside from the visitors, Bessie had her fishing to keep her occupied. Bessie did love to fish. She would wait till I'd come in every afternoon and could stay with the children, then she'd head out up the river to take off any fish she'd caught and to rebait her hooks, generally with live green frogs that she and Lovie had caught sometime during the day along the water's edge.

It was while on one of these jaunts that she came so close to getting "bear et."

A time or two, we'd seen bear tracks in the trail dust beside the river. And then one day while I was drawing water, I happened to look across the river and sight a big black bear feeding in the cane brakes on the other side. I'd taken my gun, ridden Boomer across the river, and hunted the bear till dark, but never got a shot.

Then, only a few days later, we'd listened to a panther prowling the high point across Tornillo Creek and emitting at regular intervals that peculiar, blood-chilling squawl that I rather think is the big cat's mating call.

Having seen and heard such fierce animals around home within the last few days, Bessie was quite naturally a bit nervous as she headed up the river to her catfish lines. It was nearly sundown, so that already blue dusk was darkening the narrow trail that led between a tall stand of river cane on one side and a high, rocky cliff on the other.

I was sitting on my bed out under the arbor, resting from my hard day's work and playing with Lucille, when I heard Bessie scream. She screamed again before I could get Lucille off my lap, grab up a rifle and dash out into the yard where I could see.

I looked up the river canyon. There she came, down the narrow, crooked trail, running the fastest I ever saw a woman run in my life, her screams making the whole canyon ring.

"A bear, Oscar!" she cried. "A panther!"

I swung my gun to my shoulder, and felt a cold knot form in my stomach as I realized how far away Bessie was, and what little chance I'd have to get in a killing shot at the beast that was charging her. And even if I could get a shot, I'd be shooting right toward Bessie.

But maybe I could turn the animal, I thought, and scanned the trail behind Bessie.

Watch that trail as closely as I could, however, I couldn't get a glimpse of the creature that was charging her.

Then Bessie hung her toe on a sharp ledge. She went down with even a louder scream and a clatter of the metal bait bucket she still carried. But her fall didn't stop her. Instantly, she bounded to her feet, running faster than ever, now that she'd lost her bucket.

At a sharp bend in the trail, Bessie disappeared behind a tall stand of cane. Knowing I wouldn't be able to see her again till she'd reached the mouth of Tornillo Creek, I yelled at Lovie to look after Lucille and went running down the trail that led from the house to the creek. The trail was so steep that sometimes I wasn't running at all, just jumping ten or fifteen feet down the slope, to hit sliding rock, from which I'd jump again.

[94]

When I hit level ground on the bottom of the canyon, I had up so much momentum that I almost fell flat on my face before my feet could catch up with the rest of my body.

We'd rigged up a boulder-and-log crossing above the shallow water of Tornillo Creek. I headed for it, but before I got there, here came Bessie bursting out of the cane. Without a glance at our foot-bridge, she came tearing through the shallow water, knocking sheets of it in all directions, to fall into my arms, sobbing.

"A bear, Oscar!" she cried. "A panther. I heard it splashing in the water and then it came right at me through the cane."

"Well, don't cry," I said. "You've outrun it."

As soon as I could get her calmed down a little, I went on up the trail, watching closely.

Reason told me now that the bear or panther Bessie had encountered probably hadn't charged her. More likely, the creature had been just as frightened as she. Still, a man doesn't like to have such huge animals prowling around close to home and frightening his family. It would save a lot of worry all around if I could kill the beast.

I watched the trail for tracks, just in case Bessie had been chased; but I saw only her own tracks—and bait bucket smashed flat.

A little further on, I heard it. A splash in the water, then the rustling and threshing sound that tall cane makes when some creature is forcing its way through.

I thumbed back the hammer of my rifle to full cock. I brought the stock up almost to my shoulder. Tense but ready, I crept closer —and came within a hair of shooting one of Cleofas Natividad's spotted Spanish goats as it stepped into the trail.

Other goats came out of the cane to stand and stare at me with that baffling stare that only a goat can give you. Then I heard a splash, and up the bank bounded both the herd dogs that Cleofas had trained to stay with the goats and guard them night and day.

The dogs were streaming water. They moved toward me, barking and growling, daring me to harm one of their charges. Those goats had been Bessie's "bear" or "panther."

It took Bessie a week to get over her fright so that she'd go back to her fishing.

But nothing really stopped her for long. There was the time she walked down the river bed with some of the bath guests and stepped into the quicksand.

She had been walking behind the crowd, carrying her inevitable fishing pole and bait bucket. The quicksand had supported the weight of the others, but they had tramped it until it was soft and "quicky," as she called it. She stepped in and went down past her ankles.

She called for help, and the others came back to try to pull her out. But all they could do was pull till Bessie's arms ached, and still she couldn't get loose. She began going down and down.

The way Bessie tells it, when she had sunk up to her knees, she began remembering how one of the neighbor's jersey cows had bogged in the river bed and finally died there. She thought back further, and remembered a pony that had sunk out of sight farther up the river.

Finally Bessie took the weight off her feet by leaning all the way over and lying down flat on her stomach in the sand. The quicksand stopped sucking her under then. Pulling hard, she finally loosened her feet and crawled to safety.

After that, she and the visitors took the rough, rocky trail farther up the bank along the river, rather than going the smooth way and risking the quicksand.

But they tell me that as soon as Bessie was out of the quicksand and had rested awhile, she picked up her pole and bait bucket and went on down to a pool in the river where she was almost sure to catch a fish.

Eighteen

THAT SECOND SUMMER, more than ever, we came to love and appreciate the beauty of this wild region. The location of our home on a high point gave us a view of miles of surrounding mountains, canyons, and streams. Almost every evening after the day's work was done, we'd sit outside, watching the gorgeous play of color on the mountains. As the sun set, its last rays would penetrate the purplish haze that usually shrouded the Carmens, setting fire to the range, making it glow with various hues till long after the sun had disappeared in the west.

Far below us would be the Rio Grande, its waters a shining silver in the fading light, and all around were the golden hills, with their countless broken draws and canyons filled with strange bluish shadows.

Often, during a cool, windy period we'd watch a stream of clouds many miles wide flowing across the table-top of the Carmens, spilling off down the mountainside and across the foothills. Some two thousand feet below, the cloud formation was rolled back and uplifted by a current of warm air. This ocean of clouds would completely hide the entire range from sight, flowing for hours under the bright sun with every appearance of water.

At other times, when temperature and wind direction were right, small sheets of clouds, floating lazily along this high escarpment, would be sucked down into the canyon below, where they were rolled into a huge, dense bolster of downy white. The bolster would be several hundred feet in diameter and many miles in length and would hang there in the silver light like a great dirigible anchored to a peak halfway up the golden walls of the Carmens.

There were in these sights a splendor and magnificence not to be denied. There was in them, too, that which could quiet and ease the restless spirit of man.

A great part of the fascination this country held for me lay in the signs and relics to be found yet of the peoples who'd lived here in the past, their legends, and the stories of how certain peaks and canyons had got their names.

On the rock bluffs near the upper spring are pictographs of reptiles, arrows, tomahawks, and many other strange paintings that have refused to give up their bright red color to the ravaging elements during the many years since they were painted there. In the top of a flat ledge between the two springs are several holes where in ages past Indians pounded their corn with stone *manos*, grinding the grain into meal. And all about the hills lie the old camp grounds, with their fire-blackened stones, chips of flint, with now and then a lost or discarded arrowhead to be picked up.

Juan Sada told me the legend of how the Chisos Mountains got their name. By about 1882, white men had driven most of the Big

Bend Indians into Mexico, deporting others to Indian Territory, now Oklahoma. Baja del Sol, the Apache chief who lived with his people in these mountains, realized that soon they would have to go. Reluctantly, he made a treaty with the governor of the state of Chihuahua to let his people move down into that country.

But after they had moved, Baja del Sol became homesick for his old hunter's paradise among the high peaks and longed to return. Finally, unable to endure the strange land of Mexico any longer, he selected a few of his most trusted warriors and, with their squaws, they fled back to their homeland. They traveled under cover of darkness and hid in the daytime.

At last, they reached their old range and went back to the caves they had known as home all their lives. There, they eluded the American soldiers for many months, foraging at night, holing up in the caves during the day.

Then something happened. By the time the legend got to my ears, nobody seemed to know what it was or why it had happened. But whatever brought it on, the chief's own people killed him.

And not long after Baja del Sol's death, the chief's murderers began to hear his footsteps in the mountains and even sometimes to see his ghost at night, walking restlessly across the high ridges.

And so it was that they named the range the Chisos, or Ghost Mountains.

Near Boquillas Canyon, which divides the Carmens from the Caballo Muerto Mountains, on the Texas side, is a small box canyon known as Dead Horse Canyon. From what I could learn, this canyon acquired its name through the brutal indifference of man to the suffering of his fellow creatures.

It seems that back in some early day several Brewster County ranchmen rode into Mexico, where they bought horses cheap, then attempted to smuggle them back into Texas. They crossed the Rio Grande; but before attempting to take the horses further into the country, they thought it best to check on the whereabouts of the

Texas Rangers. So they corralled the illegal horses in this small canyon, blocked up every entrance and rode away.

One of the party rode to Marathon, got a line-up on the Ranger force movements, and came back with unfavorable news. If they attempted to move those horses they were almost sure to get caught.

So, for fear of tangling with the dreaded Ranger force, they abandoned the horses, leaving them to die of starvation there in the canyon.

Nineteen

ANY TIME OUR guests failed to keep life interesting, we could depend on our neighbors to do so.

There were the Sadas, probably the most distinguished of all the Mexican families in the neighborhood. *Señor* Juan and his wife Chata had moved from the interior of Mexico in the 1870's to Boquillas, Mexico. There they opened a general merchandise store and saloon. Later they built adobe buildings and put in a stock of goods and a restaurant on the Texas side of the river.

The Sadas were a generous, warm-hearted couple; having no children of their own, they had adopted several children throughout the years. One of their adopted daughters, Flora Athade, grew up and married and soon had a son. This child, Carlito Cortez, was a frail boy who lingered near death for most of his first year of life. In their anxiety for him, Flora and Chata made a vow that if the child were allowed to live, they would send food and clothing to the poor in Boquillas, Mexico, as soon as the little one was old enough to ride a burro.

I was lucky enough to see the boy on the day Flora and Chata fulfilled their vow. Carlito was dressed in a costume the two women had copied from an old colored picture of the Santo Niño de Atoche. He wore a black hat with the brim rolled up on one side and a feather in the crown. His jacket was blue with wide white cuffs on the long sleeves. And a round, stiffly starched collar encircled the boy's neck. Under the jacket, he wore a long yellow skirt, girdled at the waist with a golden cord tasseled at the ends. On his feet were sandals. In one hand he carried a staff with the heads of wheat fastened on it, and in the other a gourd rattle.

In spite of the sacredness of the occasion, Carlito frisked about, very much pleased with his outfit. And when the burro was finally loaded with gifts, the boy was lifted onto the animal's back and he and his escort began their journey of mercy. They rode slowly down the trail, winding through the willow thickets on the bank of the river; and the thud of the burro's hoofs on the hard trail was soon silenced by the shallow silvery stream of the Rio Grande through which they waded.

It was a sight I won't soon forget.

There was a Mr. May of Alpine who used to come around to all the little villages in our neighborhood with his big tent and his crude motion picture outfit. For awhile, he had a lucrative business.

Then one fateful night, he showed his pictures at Boquillas, Mexico.

Most of the natives had never seen a moving picture, and they were enchanted. The ecstacy of the crowd reached its peak when May threw onto the screen a beautiful, green, flower-strewn valley with a bubbling stream of water flowing through it. Around the foot of a mountain rimming this valley curved a railroad, which gradually straightened out in a direct course toward the audience squatted on the ground in the tent.

Now few of these people had ever seen a train; and they sat in open-mouthed wonder when presently a passenger train, belching smoke and cinders, rounded the curve of the mountain a few miles away and rapidly grew larger as it came down the track.

At the tense moment when the train seemed to be only a few feet away, some pranking Texas cowboy let loose a ripping yell of warning: *"Cuidado, hombres!"*

This was too much. That warning to "Look out!" stampeded the crowd, which, in its wild surge to escape the train, completely wrecked May's motion picture machine and tent.

In all my time and experience spent in the Big Bend country, I have seen untold numbers of grocery and other stores opened on both sides of the border. And almost invariably these stores would run a few months and then close, usually at a small loss. It was always my private opinion that they failed at a small loss only because their owners didn't have enough cash or credit to make it possible for them to fail at a larger loss.

But the distinction of failing on the very first day their business venture was launched was earned by a couple of Mexican friends in Boquillas, Mexico.

These men had been drinking tequila in a saloon one day, paying ten cents a glass. Now they knew that tequila cost a dollar a quart; so they set about finding how many ten-cent glasses a quart held and were astonished to find that it held twenty. So! The bartender was buying a dollar bottle and selling it to customers for two dollars. That was one hundred per cent profit!

Shrewdly, the two friends put their heads and their entire cash capital together and bought two quarts of tequila. Tomorrow, they would open their own saloon. In a matter of days, they would be rich!

The next morning they hung a sign over the door of an abandoned adobe hut: *"Salón de Bebidas."* They were in business.

They considered it a good omen that the day was a bitterly cold one. On such a day, people would naturally want a little bit of something to warm them.

But the morning went by without one single customer. The two friends looked to each other for encouragement and shrugged their shoulders. This afternoon would be better, they were convinced of that.

But the afternoon was no better. The long shadows of late evening lay in the streets, and yet not one customer had crossed the threshold of the new *Salón de Bebidas*.

Finally, to ease the pain of this bitter experience, the two friends poured themselves drinks from the untouched bottles. This was so good that they poured another. Before long, then, friends dropped in; but it was after closing time now, and you do not charge a friend for a drink after closing time.

When their business was completely gone, the two friends set aside their two empty bottles and went home together to sleep off their drunk; just as they always had in the past.

Twenty

By now, my health had improved till I had more energy than good sense. Once a week, I walked to La Noria and back for our mail, a fourteen-mile round trip up and down Tornillo Creek. In heat as high as one hundred and five degrees Fahrenheit, I could easily make the round trip in a day and have time for a visit with my friend Landrum.

It was at about this time that I was appointed judge to hold the primary election there at La Noria. The appointment held little honor, since La Noria had failed to turn in its ballot boxes for years. It had long been the custom there for the losing faction in an election to break up the polls with free-for-all fist fights.

I looked the situation over and decided that this was one year we'd get the votes in to Alpine. I swore in two clerks that I felt were honest enough to take the votes fairly. Then I swore in a deputy, Jim Burtram, as peace officer. I told him to buckle on his forty-four and see to it that nobody broke up this election.

Prese..., . _gan arriving on burros, mules, horses, in buckboards, and on foot. After milling around awhile, some of them went in and voted, and some of them finally rode off without ever voting. But it was a peaceful election, with enough ballots cast to make it respectable. I was proud to take the boxes in to Alpine.

When I got back home, I began work on our house again. This time, I added two more rooms, building them out of rock and doing the work myself.

I'd watched Herman Jacobs work with stone until I felt confident that I could do it, too. And I did, although not at quite the rate of speed or with the perfection Herman achieved.

While gathering the stones from the hillsides, it came to me how useful a wheelbarrow would be. I knew it would take a long time to get to me if I ordered one; and besides, the things cost money, of which I had little. So again I improvised. I used a grindstone for a wheel, mesquite poles for the frame and handles, then added a box into which to put my stones. It worked fine and I was proud of it; but when it came to improvising gloves to keep the hot rocks from burning my hands, I wasn't quite so ingenious. The best I could do there was to drop a gunnysack over a rock before I put my hands on it. It was the hottest weather I have ever experienced, and I didn't imagine it, either. According to my government thermometer the temperature rose to 108 every day for six weeks.

Willow poles framed the roof of the new addition, and cane, covered with corrugated metal roofing, was used to shut out the heat and rain. I used stone to frame the door and windows, and poured a concrete floor for smoother walking. When I was done, we were finally able to move our kitchen stove into the house.

This was done in addition to looking after the bath-house guests. But looking after them required little time; so when I'd finished building our two rooms, I hired out to repair the school buildings at La Noria and at San Vicente. And before this work was completed, I'd been elected to serve with two other homesteaders as trustee on the school board in charge of these two school houses.

We managed to hire a teacher from East Texas to teach at La Noria, but failed to get one for the San Vicente school. As time went on and we still got no application for San Vicente, Jesse Deemer cornered me one day at La Noria.

"Why don't you resign as trustee and teach that school yourself? The job pays seven hundred dollars a year," he said.

I shook my head. "I never taught school in my life," I told Jesse.

Jesse laughed. "What of it?" he said. "Most of those kids never went to school, either. You could just all start out together."

At the moment, I rejected the idea. But later, I got to thinking about it. I needed the money. Finally, I asked myself, why not? I could read and write and figure. I'd finished high school in Jacinto, Mississippi, back in 1897. I ought to know something.

The more I studied about it, the better I liked the idea. All I had to do was go to Alpine and pass a teacher's examination, and the job would be mine.

After a few days of worrying the thing over, I made up my mind to try it. I found out when the examinations were to be held, then made arrangements to go to Marathon, where I could catch a train to Alpine.

Twenty-one

PEDRO LARA drove the mail hack between Marathon and Boquillas, and on the day that I caught a ride with him, he was breaking in a new team—a pair of wall-eyed Spanish bronc ponies. The only way they'd consent to draw the hack was to charge off at runaway speed and keep running till they gave out, then stand stock still till they were rested enough to tear out again. One bronc was fat, and we called him Prosperity; the other was thin and we named him Calamity.

Traveling by fits and starts, with Pedro and me both holding the reins most of the time, we easily covered the eighty-five miles to Marathon in two days.

But by the time we'd got there, I'd lost my courage about the teacher's examination. I had no idea what it would be like, and I felt now that I couldn't hope to pass it. All I'd do would be to go up to Alpine and make a fool of myself. The more I thought about it, the more reluctant I became.

When it finally came right down to buying my train ticket to

Alpine, I just couldn't do it. I helped Pedro load the buckboard with the mail and provisions he'd come for; then I got in with him and we headed back toward the Rio Grande. I felt like a fool, but not quite as big a fool as I knew I'd feel after I'd tried those examinations.

By now, Calamity and Prosperity had worn the keen edge off their enthusiasm for running and we were able to proceed with the two working somewhat as a team. That is, when they broke and ran, they at least ran together, making it easier for us to keep them somewhere near the road and to guide them around the bigger rocks and brush thickets.

Soon after we left Marathon, rain began falling on us and continued to fall all day long. We had planned to camp that night at Midway, just south of Maravillas Creek, forty miles from Marathon. But when we arrived at the creek just about dark, we found it flooded, with the water spreading all over the valley where we'd planned on camping.

We managed to halt Calamity and Prosperity at the edge of the water, where they stood with their necks craned around so they could stare at us, their eyes showing a lot of white and their nostrils flared. We talked the matter over and decided that the water wouldn't be too deep to cross, but that maybe we'd better swing around and go back about a hundred yards and take a run at it so we wouldn't get stuck in the middle. With a little speed, we figured we ought to cross without any great trouble.

Throughout the trip up to now, all our efforts had gone into holding back the team. Now, however, after we'd swung them around and headed toward the water again, we turned them wild loose and started hollering. This proved to be almost more than the team could stand. They snorted and left out, running like a pair of frightened jackrabbits. The buckboard rocked and wallowed like a boat in heavy seas. The whizzing wheels picked up mud and slung it ten feet high in a continuous shower.

The ponies took to that first stretch of shallow, muddy water at a dead run. They knocked sheets of water in all directions, some of it even flying back in our faces so that we couldn't see. Pedro and I whooped and yelled at the team, urging them on. Just ahead was the main creek current, rolling high in the middle, but narrow. One quick lunge in and out of it, and we'd be across.

Suddenly Prosperity and Calamity threw all feet forward and squatted, nearly throwing Pedro and me out over the dashboard. Even braced as they were, they slid forward a little before they stopped. But stop they did, right at the edge of that high-rolling main current. And there they stood.

We hollered at them. We swore at them. Pedro reached down and picked up a blacksnake whip and went to using it.

But it was no use. Prosperity and Calamity had gone as far as they meant to go. I could see that in their white-rolling eyes when each of them swung his head around to stare back at us. They'd flinch when we hollered at them. Under Pedro's lash, they'd snort and groan and rear and try to turn crossways in their harness.

But nothing was making them move one step forward.

We waited awhile, thinking maybe they'd just run themselves down and needed a rest. But no go. We waited longer, hoping that after awhile the creek itself would run down and then we could persuade them to cross. But the creek didn't run down. Instead, it rose higher. By good dark, it was up above the hubs of the wagon wheels.

By midnight, it was pouring through the buckboard bed.

And still the rain poured on. Great jagged streaks of lightning speared the blackness, illuminating the rain-washed world from horizon to horizon. Then suddenly the light chopped off, leaving us in darkness as black as the inside of a cow. A moment later would come the thunderclap, so violent that it shook the very earth under our buckboard.

But none of this stirred Prosperity and Calamity. They stood right there on the side of the main current. And some time in the night, they turned completely around in the harness to face us with their heads down and their tails tucked, while the rain streamed down over their backs.

Finally, as wet and miserable as we were there in the spring-seat, Pedro and I slept.

We awoke at sunrise to a sight that shook us both. At last, the creek had run down. And there, just ahead of Prosperity and Calamity, so close that their feet were crumbling the edges of it, yawned a monstrous hole in the creek.

Gingerly, we got out and inspected it. Some trick of the flood had started a whirlpool here that had undercut the bank and eaten down into the bed of the creek. It was nearly six feet straight down to the water level now and the water looked to be four or five feet deep.

We looked at Prosperity and Calamity. They stared back at us and rolled their eyes. And then Pedro looked at me and crossed himself and said *"Santo Cristo!"* in a breathless voice, and I breathed the prayer after him.

But for the sagacity or intuition of our wild-eyed runaway broncs, none of us would have been alive this morning.

From the north, another rain cloud was bearing down on us, a great black tumbling mass, with streaks of lightning ripping across the face of it.

We looked at the cloud and considered our predicament. We could go downstream and cross the Maravillas before it flooded again. But what about the Tornillo? There'd be no crossing it for hours after this second rain fell. Maybe not for days. The prospect of waiting, waterbound, out here in the great wide open for a day or so, with no bedding, no drinking water, and very little food, didn't appeal to us. The best thing we could do, we decided, was to head back for Marathon.

We put a nose twist on each of our wild broncs, just to make sure they didn't change their minds now and maybe plunge off into the whirlpool hole in front of them. We straightened their harness and led them around till they were headed back in the direction we'd come. We climbed into the buckboard, spoke to them, and left out for Marathon again at the same runaway pace that we'd traveled this whole trip.

Once back in town, I think it was lack of anything else to do that finally made me catch a train to Alpine. I reasoned that if we were going to have to wait around here for a day or so till the rains stopped, then I might just as well spend my time taking that teacher's examination as watching the weather.

I was one of three who arrived at the Alpine high school building the next morning to take the examination. The other two were a young lady and a youngster from Fort Stockton who'd finished high school only the year before. They looked as nervous as I felt.

We all felt even more nervous when the cigar-smoking superintendent of the school came in and wrote our first questions on the blackboard. I can't remember now what the questions were, but I can remember how empty and helpless I felt when I read them. I didn't know the answer to a one.

I sat and doodled and squirmed in my seat. I glanced over at the other two applicants and found them doing the same thing. When I looked up at the superintendent, I found him staring moodily at the end of his half-smoked cigar.

A moment later, as if he'd finally made up his mind about something, he jerked to his feet, went over to an open window and flung his cigar outside.

"I've got to go uptown and get me another cigar," he announced. "I may be gone a couple of hours. The library's in the next room."

He got his hat and left then. I turned and looked at the other two applicants. They sat and looked back at me. Then we all grinned and got up and went into the library and went to work.

By the time the superintendent came back with a fresh cigar, we had all the answers to those first questions written out and were ready for the next set.

It took us two days to complete that examination. But with the aid of a library and a superintendent who was constantly having to go to town for more cigars, we all passed with flying colors.

In fact, I made such a high grade that I came out with a four-year school teaching certificate, instead of the two-year one that I had expected to get.

I don't know what finally became of Pedro's bronc ponies, Calamity and Prosperity. But I've always had a warm place in my heart for them since that trip. Not only did they save my life, but they were instrumental in my earning a badly needed seven hundred dollars as a school teacher that next year.

Twenty-two

It was some five miles up the Rio Grande from our place to the little school house at San Vicente. Night and morning for the next ten months, I walked the old rough river trail beaten out by the Indians long before white men ever came to this continent. And felt the better for the walk.

Sometimes I left the trail to search the creek banks and canyon slopes for arrowheads or interesting geological formations. In those days, arrowheads were to be found by the dozens around old campgrounds of the Comanche, Lipan, Kickapoo, and Apache, the tribes which once held this section. It was not uncommon either to find water *ollas* in perfect state of preservation, and *metates* and *manos* that the Indians had used to grind their corn. Then, in the draws, where the water had worn away the soil, I often came across wonderful specimens of fossils, such as nautilites, ammonites, and trilobites. These I collected as I found them and kept carrying them home till our house began to take on the appearance of a museum.

Each morning, on my way to school, I found tracks in the trail dust to show what wild creatures had used the trail during the night—raccoons, ring-tail cats, skunks, coyotes, badgers. Once I saw the tracks of a huge panther; another time, those of a bear.

In the afternoons, there'd be the tracks of the burros or horses ridden by men who'd traveled the trail during the day.

Then there were often ducks feeding in the still pools of the Rio Grande; sometimes swallows building their mud nests against the high walls; a kingfisher hurtling himself into the water with a chattering cry and coming up with a struggling fish. One day I saw an eagle flying up the river canyon with a wriggling snake in its talons.

There were the thick cottony fogs that sometimes hung low in the canyons till long after sunup, so that when I walked in a low place, I could see nothing above; or, topping out a high rise, I'd find myself moving across a strange world that was only a small island set in the midst of a white sea.

Once I came upon a thing I'd never seen before—a rattlesnake swallowing a rabbit.

He was a huge diamondback, lying under a greasewood bush beside the trail, in a gravelly *arroyo* wash. In his mouth, which was distended to impossible proportions, it seemed to me, was a cottontail rabbit, already swallowed down past its shoulders and forefeet. Around the rest of the rabbit's body, the snake was wound in tight coils.

I stood and watched for awhile. With a convulsive movement, the rattler would jerk his coils tighter, crushing the rabbit's body and forcing more of it into his mouth. After that, he'd lie and rest awhile, then try again.

Finally, I started searching for a weapon with which to kill the snake. But there was nothing around, no rocks or anything heavy enough to use as a club. At last, I broke off the dead stem of a greasewood bush that I thought might do, and rapped the snake across the head. But my club was too light; it broke in my hands without even making a mark on the reptile.

The blow did, however, make the big rattler unwind his coils and disgorge the dead rabbit. With what was left of my stick, I tried to fight the snake away from a nearby gopher hole; but I had no luck. Rattles singing angrily, he came right on toward me, forcing me to give ground. He crawled on into the hole, with me still whipping him with the stick.

The next morning, the dead rabbit was gone, but the soil there was too hard and gravelly for me to tell whether the rattler had come back and got it, or if possibly a coon or coyote had stolen it from the snake.

But even more interesting than my walks were my school and pupils. The school house itself was a single room of adobe, roofed with shingles. It had a fireplace in one end, a door in the opposite end, and two glass windows on either side. It sat on a high dirt bank, overlooking a bend in the Rio Grande, and afforded a good view of the old Spanish fort of San Vicente and the lonesome, hazy, gaping canyons that separated the bare ridges and peaks of the rugged San Vicente Mountains across the river.

From the school house a little trail wound down through a break in the bluff to the river, where several times a day we filled the brass-bound cedar bucket that held drinking water for the students.

Some thirty children enrolled the first day, all of them clean, neatly dressed, and eager. Of these, a few of the older ones could speak a little English. Some could even read a bit in the primer. But the rest could neither speak nor understand a word of English.

Since I could speak almost no Spanish, I was at first pretty baffled as to how to go about teaching anything. But the older pupils came to my rescue. When I spoke a sentence, they'd immediately translate it into Spanish for the younger ones. And I must confess that I am still amazed at how fast my pupils caught on. Starting out in a foreign language, some of those little ones had completely mastered the primer long before the ten-month term was up. They learned the alphabet, recognized each letter, read in English, and knew the meaning of what they read.

One older boy, who had spent ten years herding goats, learned his letters in two or three days, started reading before the week was out, and by the end of the third week, had read the entire primer.

Simón, son of Cleofas Natividad, was another promising student. He, too, had spent most of his young life herding goats, rather than going to school. But he quickly learned to read and write, kept it up after he finished school, and within the next few years acquired sufficient knowledge and understanding to become pastor of a Baptist church in Midland, Texas.

Even more amazing was the ability of those youngsters to draw and to write. They seemed born with that artistic coordination between hand and eye that allowed them to copy exactly what they saw. Almost as soon as any of them learned to write, they wrote a much more beautiful and readable hand than I did. And when it came to drawing pictures, they just knew how, at the start. They'd come to the blackboard, think for a moment, then draw a donkey loaded with wood, or a rooster chasing a grasshopper, or a goat reared up to eat the leaves out of a bush. And in almost every case, they'd automatically put in that certain intangible something that brought the picture alive.

And there was no faltering, no erasing and starting over. They might stop and study a moment or two before they began; but once started, they executed the chalk strokes with all the sureness of a trained artist.

On the school grounds, they enjoyed their games even more, it seemed, than the usual run of Anglo-American children. They played bull-pen, ante-over, and baseball. They argued little, almost never fought, and seemed cheerfully willing to obey my slightest command or reprimand without argument or resentment.

The only exception was the time a difference occurred between a little girl and a much older boy, who deliberately punched her in the eye with his finger.

All the children seemed indignant at this cruel act; but when I whipped the boy, they didn't like that, either. The first rap brought a spontaneous murmur which reminded me of angry bees buzzing. The murmur grew louder as the whipping continued. And then, when it was over, there was a dead silence.

That silence, plus looks of reproach, was about the only response I got to my attempts at teaching for the rest of that day. And the next morning, I found that during my absence, the blackboard had been slashed with a knife.

Not quite sure what to do about that, I did nothing. Which, apparently, was the proper course to take. Nothing more came of the incident and, fortunately, I was never faced with a like situation again.

As a teacher, I take no credit for the way my pupils learned or for their good conduct. I was about the sort of teacher you might expect me to have been, with my limited education and total lack of experience. My pupils didn't learn good manners from me; they had good manners when they came to school. They didn't learn arf from me; they were born with an instinctive knowledge. And as for what they learned about reading and writing, they learned that from me only because I showed them how to learn a thing they were eager to learn.

For me, those children made teaching a real pleasure.

Twenty-three

IT WAS THAT FALL, not long after my school had started in September, that the meteor fell. At least, I suppose it was a meteor, although I'll probably never know with complete certainty just what terrible phenomenon of nature caused us that awful fright in the night.

The weather was still hot. I never liked to sleep in the house during hot weather; so I had a bedstead and mattress under the river-cane arbor on the east side of the house. We always got a good cool breeze here, and almost never did the mosquitoes come that high up out of the Rio Grande canyon.

On this night, Lovie and I were sleeping outside; Bessie and the baby slept in the house. It was sometime after midnight that I started awake to find the world about us illuminated by a great white light, and the air filled with an awful cracking and rumbling, as if whole mountains were breaking apart and tumbling down.

Without even thinking what I was doing, I leaped out of bed

and ran out into the open yard. Behind me, I heard Lovie cry out. "Daddy!" she screamed and came running to cling to me. And then here came Bessie, clutching the baby in her arms, her frightened face plainly visible in the great light.

"Oscar!" she cried. "What it is, Oscar?"

And of course, I couldn't answer her. I didn't know what it was and was probably too terrified to talk if I'd had the answer. All I could do was hold Lovie in one arm and pat Bessie on the shoulder with the other hand and stare out at a world that was surely coming to an end.

Cowering against the house, Tex lifted her nose and howled in a way that made cold shivers run up my spine. I was conscious, too, of the rooster crowing and crowing again, and from out at the little corral I'd made for Boomer came the sounds of his frightened snorting and lunging, then finally a wild braying.

How long the light and sound lasted, I don't know. Evidently, for half a minute, at least. For I recollect looking out over the great gash of the Rio Grande and seeing in minute detail every rock and crevice and ripple on the water and every hill and bush and rocky ravine, clear to the blazing face of the Carmen Mountains. It was the same when I looked south toward the San Vicente Mountains. Every feature of the land stood out in bold detail, illuminated by a light that was brighter and more glaring than a noonday sun.

The light and sound seemingly had no source; it was just there, all about us, making us quake with fear.

Then, suddenly, there was a greater sound, like some sort of terrific explosion. The light flared brighter, reached an almost blinding intensity, then went out, leaving us in total darkness. While we stood blinking in the dark, successive waves of sound slammed up against the Carmens, rolled back to go rumbling up the Rio Grande till they struck the San Vicente Mountains, then returned down the Rio Grande, slamming and banging against the canyon walls again.

It all happened so quickly and was so terrifying that, when the sun rose the next morning, Bessie and I could hardly believe it had happened. It was more like some hideous nightmare that you want to forget as quickly as possible.

But nightmarish as it had seemed, there'd been more substance to it than a bad dream. José Díaz, a rancher from across the river in Mexico, had seen it, and came down to the house the next morning, still alarmed.

"It is a fact, *Señor*," he said in a voice of awe, "that the very earth shook beneath my feet!"

Later, I learned that others had heard the sound and seen the light clear beyond Persimmon Gap in the Santiago Range forty miles to the north.

Some fifteen years later, I ran across the only explanation I ever found for the thing that happened that night. I was exploring some Indian campgrounds in the foothills of the Carmens for artifacts, and my guide, Juan Luna, led me to a great hole in the earth some five or six miles from Boquillas. It was a great bowl-shaped depression, something like a hundred feet in diameter and possibly half that deep, with pulverized dirt and broken rock rimming the edges.

If it was a meteor that made that terrible light and sound that night, then I'm convinced that the crater Juan Luna showed me is its resting place.

Twenty-four

A TRAVELER FROM SAN VICENTE brought me the sad news. My
friend Gregorio Marufo had lost his son.

The traveler was philosophical. He pointed out that in San Vicente Gregorio was a man of importance. He lived in a fine rock
house of two rooms. He owned a big farm. He owned many goats.
He owned many chickens. Almost never was he without a pig fat-
tening in the sty he'd dug into the ground near his house.

But disease had struck down Gregorio's strong husky son the
same as if he'd never had enough to eat. It had shut off his water,
so that he could not urinate; and he'd swelled and swelled until he
could no longer stand the pain.

And now, my informant concluded, the boy was just as dead as
if he had been the son of a poor man.

That evening I walked to San Vicente to attend the funeral. I arrived a bit late, so that most of the people from San Vicente were

already there. They stood silent, with eyes downcast, as I walked through them toward the house.

The corpse was laid out on a bench under the brush arbor in front of Gregorio's house. There was a white cotton sheet on the bench, then one spread over the body. Around the corpse were dozens of slow burning candles of goat tallow.

I walked past the body and extended my hand to Gregorio, who came to meet me at the door. My friend shed no tears as he looked at me, but deep in his eyes I could see a flood of them held in check. At the proper time they would flow; that was plain by the sorrow and despair that showed in the deep lines of his weathered face.

He took my hand and said: "*Señor,* my son is dead," then turned from me and went back into the house.

I left the door to stand silently among the others till the village *jefe,* Comillo Celaya, arrived with a pistol in his hand. Now the funeral procession was ready to start.

Adolfo Yarte, Ysidro Sanchez, Juan Gamboa, and Fermin Salas, close friends of my friend Gregorio, were the bearers. They came with a litter, made of cottonwood poles and a woolen blanket, and laid it on the ground beside the corpse. Gently, they lifted the stiffened body, still covered by the sheet, and placed it upon the litter. Then, one at each of the four corners, they lifted the litter to their shoulders and stood waiting.

Outside, the *jefe* raised his revolver till the muzzle pointed skyward toward the brilliant afterglow of the setting sun, and squeezed the trigger.

The short flat report was a shocking sound in the vast silence of the Rio Grande valley.

The litter bearers moved out. Behind them, a long double queue formed, the immediate family coming first, close friends next, then neighbors and acquaintances. Last came the *jefe* with the gun in his hand. Together, in solemn procession, we moved to-

[123]

ward the *campo santo*, the sainted field, where the grave had already been dug.

There was no talk, even in whispers. There were no cries of anguish, no lamentations. Even the scrape and shuffle of our feet on the loose gravelly soil seemed muted in the presence of death.

Crashing into this hushed quietness came the report of the revolver again. I felt my nerves tighten. Ahead of me, I saw some of my friends flinch, almost as if the bullet had struck them. But that was all. They uttered no sound. The echoes of the report ran shouting across the wide valley and quickly lost themselves in the surrounding hills and *arroyos*. Then the silence was more intense than ever.

Six times, at regular intervals, in that half-mile trip, the gun was fired; the last time, just as the litter-bearers reached the grave. Then the line broke and the mourners came to stand quietly around the gaping hole and the mound of raw earth beside it.

There were no hymns sung, no prayers uttered. There was no weeping, no suppressed sobs of grief. Just silence.

Four men slid into the open grave to receive the litter from the bearers. Carefully, they lowered the sheet-wrapped body to its resting place. They removed the litter, handed it up, placed a board across the head of the dead boy, then climbed out of the grave.

Gregorio Marufo, as head of the bereaved family, moved to the mound of loose soil, caught up a handful, and sifted it through his fingers over the body of his son. He moved aside. His wife caught up a handful of the soil and spilled it gently into the grave as she moved along, making room for the others of her family.

One by one, each relative, friend, and neighbor walked past the grave and performed this last rite. Then we stood back while four men shoveled dirt into the grave.

It was possibly one-third full when one of the workmen nodded to the others, then all stood back. Juan Ochoa, the biggest and strongest man in the village, came forward. He stepped down into the grave and reached for a round boulder that rested at the brink of the opening. The boulder was huge, and of such great weight that it seemed impossible that even Juan Ochoa could lift it. But lift it he did, higher than his head, then let it drop into the loose soil at his feet.

He bent and lifted it and let it drop again, time after time, each time in a new place. Sweat broke out on his swarthy face and ran down his cheeks. The great muscles of his shoulders began to tremble and quiver from the strain of his effort. But he never stopped until the boulder had been dropped on every square inch of loose soil in the grave, packing it tightly around the body of Gregorio's son.

At last, he heaved himself out. The shovelers went back to work again, piling in more dirt. And again, Juan Ochoa packed the dirt down with the great boulder.

Three times Juan Ochoa went back into the grave to pack the earth over the body of his friend before the grave was filled and rounded over. Then, still without a word, the group turned from the grave and began searching the surrounding low hills and dry *arroyos* for stones to cover the mound. The men brought big stones, the women lesser ones, and the children brought the smallest of all, some no bigger than the stones they might remove from a pan of *frijoles* their mothers would cook. In solemn silence, everyone brought stones and heaped them onto the grave till no bit of raw earth was left exposed.

A cross was stuck into the ground at the head of the grave—two short lengths of cottonwood lashed together with rawhide.

Now, at last, Gregorio Marufo's son was buried. Now, the silence could be broken. Now, the dammed-up anguish of spirit, the restrained tears of grief could pour out.

It started with a high keening wail as my friend Gregorio sank slowly to his knees and then leaned forward to grip the earth with his hands and let his head droop between his shoulders.

[125]

His wife sank down beside him, her cries rising above his. And then in little groups of twos and threes, the others followed them to the ground, some to kneel and others to squat upon their heels, while all wailed their loss and cried out in protest to the great, universal, unknown god of death.

Their lamentations filled the valley that was now darkening with purple shadows. Some became overwrought and flailed the air with their hands. Others threw themselves face down upon the ground and writhed with a frenzy of grief and impotence.

After a time, the sounds died away, however, and the tears ceased to flow. Those who had fallen to the ground now rose and stood silent and waiting until all were done with their grief. Then, just as quietly as we'd come, we moved in a group back to the house of Gregorio where, without a word, we pressed his hand again, then went away.

My friend Gregorio's son had died and now he was buried.

Twenty-five

A FEW BLACKTAIL DEER inhabited the hills and *arroyos* near our cabin and occasionally I hunted them, both for the sport and for the chance of adding meat to our larder.

"But you've never been on a real deer hunt," my friend C. L. Hannold insisted, "until you've hunted those little Sonora fantails up in the Chisos."

Hannold lived on a homestead some four miles up Tornillo Creek from me and enjoyed the reputation of being the best deer hunter in the Big Bend. So that fall when he invited me to accompany him on a week-end hunt into the Chisos, I went, more for the chance to explore those fantastic mountains than with any hopes of killing a deer.

We drove to the mountains in a buckboard loaded with our

camping plunder, guns, and ammunition. We pitched camp at a spring in Wade Canyon, one of the most picturesque spots of the Chisos. The canyon is in the shape of a great inverted horseshoe, wedged in between sheer rock walls and lofty peaks which towered high above us.

Hannold insisted that we eat lunch before taking to the woods, and we did; but I could hardly eat for staring about at the strange trees growing around us. Here, cut off from all other such trees by hundreds of miles of rolling land, were live oaks, red oaks, weeping juniper, Douglas fir, Arizona cypress, yellow pine, mountain maple, madroña and many others that I could not name. Where did they come from, I asked myself. How did they ever get here?

Hannold was more concerned about the little Sonora fantail deer that inhabit these altitudes.

"They never come down out of the high places," he said. "And they won't let a blacktail come up where they are. They run him out. The biggest kind of a fantail won't weigh more than eighty or ninety pounds, while a blacktail may run better than two hundred. But size doesn't seem to count. Let a fantail catch a blacktail too high up these slopes, and he'll run in under the bigger deer, horning him in the flanks and belly till the blacktail can't stand it. And back down to the low country he heads."

As Hannold talked, I gradually became more interested in this curious little deer. By the time we'd finished eating, I was nearly as anxious as Hannold was to kill a buck.

We hobbled out our horses, loaded our rifles, and started up a well-worn trail that led up the main *arroyo* past camp. And then I started looking again—at the majestic bare walls of the cliffs and spires above us, with their lovely gray lichen; at the emerald green of an occasional graceful piñon, clinging miraculously to a fragment of earth caught in a crevice; at the giant evergreens out on top, tall dark silhouettes against the crystal blue of the sky.

We saw an eagle, a number of ant-eating woodpeckers, one

Rocky Mountain bluebird, and blue quail by the hundreds. With a shotgun, I'd have had some wonderful shooting, right at camp; but now I was hunting deer.

Ahead, I kept hearing the roar of water, and finally we came to a great waterfall that spilled a white plume almost straight down from some hidden spring a hundred feet above.

We separated there, Hannold preferring to hunt in that section of the horseshoe that curved north and back toward camp, while I turned left up a steep slope that would take me up higher into the timber.

After something like an hour's climb, stumbling and crawling over loose rock, I reached a gap in the wall several hundred feet long, where I could look out over a vast sea of sun-bathed clouds. There were ragged holes in the clouds, through which I could catch glimpses of the desert land, thousands of feet below.

I paused, taking in the beauty of the scene, while I got my breath, then moved on.

My first glimpse of a deer was only momentary. There was a sudden snort and clatter of hoofs, but all I got to see was a flash of white disappearing over the rim of a hill.

He was too far away to follow; so I turned back toward camp, hoping that a little oak grove ahead would yield more deer.

And it did. Suddenly a six-point buck leaped from the thicket and bounded away, directly toward camp. I shot and missed, shot again and missed a second time. Then the fleet little animal was gone, and all I had for my trouble was the startled echoes, crashing back and forth between the canyon walls, multiplying as they grew fainter, till it sounded as though a hundred shots had been fired.

Then a most unexpected thing happened. The little buck gained the top of a ridge some three hundred yards away and, instead of going over and out of sight, he stepped out in plain view of me, looking back over his shoulder.

This was my chance. Probably my last one. I hadn't been a good enough shot to get him running, but if he'd hold there, broadside, for a just a moment longer . . .

I dropped to one knee, rested my elbow on the other, and brought my sights to bear on a spot just about where his heart should be. I squeezed the trigger.

Again the savage echoes ripped the silence apart and went slamming and banging through the peaks. But this time, I'd got meat. My little buck dropped as if hit in the head with a sledge-hammer.

He was a good one, fat and sleek, although the smallest grown deer that I'd ever killed. I gutted him and swung him high and far out on the limb of a juniper, where panthers or bears couldn't get to him. I was only a few hundred yards from camp, but by the very nature of the terrain, I knew it would be long after dark before I reached it.

The moon was up, slanting long bars of silver light into the canyons, when I reached camp, feeling as triumphant as hunters usually do after making a kill.

"Well," I summed up, after giving Hannold a detailed narration of my adventure, "this is the first time I ever shot a buck above the clouds."

On a later deer hunt across the Rio Grande into Mexico my luck was not so good.

This time, I went with Jim Griffin from the Texas Panhandle, who'd come down to bathe at the spring and court Hannold's daughter.

We hunted in El Jardín country, a great valley some ten miles wide, extending from the Rio Grande along the west side of the Carmens to a point some forty miles south. This is a well-watered section of a rather barren country, the rainfall coming from clouds moving in from the east and jamming up against the mountains, where they become cool and spill out their moisture. Rain falls every few days. The grass grows green here, among many varieties of herbs and shrubs that deer feed on. As a consequence, this section has some of the best hunting in northern Mexico.

At the same time, it is open country, which makes it difficult for a hunter to get within shooting distance of the wily blacktail that can see as far as any man and smell much farther.

With so much country to cover, I was advised by my Mexican cook and wagoner, Juan Athade, to hunt horseback. So I rode out that morning, fully determined to take back home the biggest rack of blacktail antlers that ever graced our cabin.

Blue quail were everywhere, sometimes as many as thirty or forty in a covey. And while most of them ran from me, ducking into patches of brush or even into prairie-dog holes, one finally did take to the air. And that's when I witnessed for the first time the curious manner in which a blue quail escapes a hawk.

The hawk, apparently unconcerned about me and my horse, swooped down upon the quail the instant the quail left the ground. And being faster on the wing, the hawk was soon upon its prey, reaching for it with open claws.

Then, at the last possible instant before he was captured, the quail did a curious thing. Instead of sailing on out as it had started, it shot suddenly straight up, letting the hawk shoot past, under it; and the quail wheeled off in another direction. Before the swiftly flying hawk could cut his speed enough to come about and give chase again, the quail was back on the ground and out of sight.

Soon after, I located my buck, with the sort of antlers I was looking for. He stood down in a little draw, with his head up in a wary, attentive manner, as if suspecting my presence but not certain yet where I was.

I cut down on him and he fell. But instantly, he was up and bounding over the next rise ahead. I spurred after him, reached the top of the rise, and was unable to see him anywhere. I wondered where he could have gone, and rode on, watchful, suspecting that he'd lain down. And sure enough, he had. Up he came, from behind a shrub, leaping away again.

I slid from my horse and cut down on him a second time. I piled him. He didn't get up. Quickly, I mounted and rode toward him.

Then up he came again, running as hard as ever. Again I shot and again he went down. And again I chased him up.

This went on until I finally lost my buck.

When I told Jim Griffin about my hard luck, back in camp, he was impatient with me.

"Why didn't you just let him lie still for a few minutes? If you'd let him bleed and stiffen, you'd have got him without any trouble."

I felt foolish. I'd never thought of that, and I made up my mind that the next time I knocked a deer down, I'd give him that chance.

But curiously enough, every time afterward that I hunted in El Jardín, "something happened," so that I lost my buck. Every incident was logical and explainable enough; yet the fact remains that never did I bring even a small set of blacktail antlers out of Mexico.

Twenty-six

By THIS TIME, I was the unofficial doctor in the community. Whenever anyone got sick and couldn't get a doctor or afford to get one, they called me in.

I remember one Saturday morning, Juan Gamboa hurried his plodding mule to our house to tell me that his little daughter Benigna had been badly burned. Would I please come? Benigna was in much pain.

The Gamboas lived a few miles away, on the Mexican side of the river. I saddled Boomer, packed up a small bundle of clean white cloths, some ointment, and some tape. Then we set out.

It took us over an hour to get to the Gamboas' home, and from the hurry Juan seemed to be in, I assumed that the child had just been burned. But when I got there, I was dismayed to learn that it had been two or three days since a kerosene can had exploded and burned Benigna.

And in the meantime, nothing had been done to relieve the girl's suffering or to prevent infection. She lay on a bare plank now, with a piece of colored tissue paper covering the burned area of her body. Her mother sat by her, constantly fanning her to keep a swarm of flies off. But that was all the medical treatment she had received since she'd been burned.

Now her right leg was drawn back and stiff. I asked the mother to heat me a little water; then I gave the child a tepid bath to clean off the big wound. I knew that would be painful to the little girl, but I knew, too, that it was necessary. And she stood it without a whimper.

After that, I gave the mother the ointment and told her to keep it on the wound and to keep it covered with the clean cloths I had brought, except for the times when I would want her to sunbathe it. Then I told *Señora* Gamboa how to do that, exposing the wound to the early morning and late afternoon sun for as long as thirty minutes at a time.

"And while Benigna is in the sun, with the dressing off her burn," I told *Señora* Gamboa, "I want you to rub that leg very gently and work it back and forth so it won't be left stiff."

Boomer and I went home, then; but somehow I didn't feel happy about the little girl. That burned leg might heal stiff and leave her a cripple. Or *Señora* Gamboa might disregard my instructions and let the wound get infected. As large an area as that burn covered, it could easily kill the child if it became badly infected.

Mentally, I sighed. I knew the only way for me to be sure that everything went right for Benigna Gamboa was to visit their home every day for awhile.

I talked to Bessie about the child and her chances for getting well when I got home.

"Oscar, a doctor came in while you were gone. He's here for the baths. Why don't you talk to him?" she suggested.

I went down and talked to the man and was gratified when he endorsed the sun treatments I had prescribed.

"If you're going back any time soon," he offered, "I can give you some pretty good burn ointment and plenty of dressings to keep the wound clean."

I took them with me when I went back the next day, along with the mattress and linen which Bessie had insisted that I take. I felt that the child was probably more comfortable on the plank bed she'd been accustomed to all her life than she would be on one of our mattresses; but Bessie couldn't stand the thought of that. So Boomer and I paid our second visit.

This time I found Benigna already much improved. *Señora* Gamboa was following my instructions to the letter. I gave her the mattress and medicine and dressings, visited a while, then came on back home.

Since I was teaching school, I couldn't make the trip to the Gamboa home except on weekends. But I didn't have to make more than one or two more trips before the burn was healed and the child's leg was functioning normally.

I couldn't have been any prouder of a doctor's certificate than I was of the sight of that little girl running and playing again.

Twenty-seven

AT THE TIME that I built our bath house over the hot spring the *Alpine Avalanche* ran a little news story that told of our improved facilities for taking care of bathers. Other newspapers in the state, such as the *Dallas News* and the *San Antonio Express,* picked up the story. From that, and from word-of-mouth advertising, the best of all, the news spread all over the state; and soon our business doubled, then tripled.

As shady camping space was limited, I was forced to build brush and cane arbors to take care of the additional visitors. Also, I went down to the lower spring, cleaned it out, built a concrete tub to catch the water, and was now able to get some returns from my lease money.

The Fort Stockton man who had filed on the hot spring land too late to get it continued to be resentful of my possession, and kept spreading stories calculated either to scare me away or to check the flow of visitors. He continued putting out scare stories of this one and that one who had been murdered along the border there. He predicted that such would eventually happen to my family, the inference being that nobody but a fool or a man who cared nothing for his family would subject them to such risks.

He scoffed, too, at the idea of the mineral springs having any curative power, and inferred that I was a fraud and a quack for taking pay from the bathers who came to be cured.

Once he came down to the spring and, under an assumed name, tried to buy it from me.

I couldn't help being upset and angry at the man when I thought about his campaign against me. But none of us was murdered, and there were too many known cases of complete cures of gonorrhea and eczema, malaria, stomach illnesses, and kidney ailments for me to pay much attention to my detractor.

There was the remarkable case of the banker from Oklahoma City. When he arrived at the spring, he was covered from head to foot with the worst case of eczema I ever saw. The only portions of his body not ravaged by the disease were those exposed to the open air, his hands and face. He was a wealthy man, and he told me that he had been under the care of various skin specialists for years, with no apparent benefits. He admitted that he had come to the spring as a last resort, and was quite frankly skeptical that it would help him.

Yet at the end of three weeks, the banker departed, the only sign left of his disease being a few little red scars not yet healed. And he didn't need to come back either. He wrote me later that he was permanently cured.

He even went so far as to recommend the spring to other people. He sent down one woman from Longview, Texas, who was in a worse shape, if possible, than he had been. Her skin was in such a raw state that she could hardly touch anything, and had to be looked after by a special nurse all the time. But after she began taking the baths, that diseased skin began peeling away, so that, by the time she had completed the full course of twenty-one baths, she was able to leave, completely healed.

There was a West Texas doctor who was so convinced of the spring's healing qualities that when his own baby contracted pneumonia, he hurried it down to the spring as fast as he could make the trip. Then he proceeded to duck the baby in the hot water, time after time. I got scared that the man was deranged with fear for his child's life. He'd hold the baby under water until the child started to strangle, then bring it up for air. I felt sure that he'd drown the baby. But he explained that what he wanted was to force the baby to suck some of the water into its lungs and nasal passages. And, either he knew what he was talking about or the baby got well in spite of the treatment. At the end of two or three weeks of bathing the baby and giving it the spring water to drink, the doctor took the child home, well again.

Later, another doctor started sending me all the old chronic cases of gonorrhea that he was unable to cure himself. I kept a special tub for these patients and let no one else bathe in it; nor would I allow the infected ones to bathe in any of the other tubs. And, so far as I know, there was never a gonorrhea patient who stayed for the full number of baths who didn't leave rid of the disease.

With such cures building up the reputation of the spring, visitors continued to come and our business grew.

And with the business growing in this manner, I was relieved of the financial strain I'd labored under for so long. That third summer, Bessie and the children made their first trip away from the homestead since we'd moved onto it; they went to Fort Worth to visit Bessie's mother. And by now I had the money to hire Mexican laborers to improve the roads and trails leading to the hot springs and to the house. I built more arbors, a shed over the lower spring and when the following May came around, I still had money for my land payments.

[138]

The land wasn't paid out, of course, and wouldn't be for years and years. But now, after three years of residence and the required improvements on the place, I could get a deed to it.

And now that the land was ours, we could leave it any time we wanted to and still hold it. But we had no notion of leaving now. Our home was here. It was here that I'd regained my health and found a full measure of happiness. The spring and my school teaching job were providing me and my family with an ample, if not luxurious, living. We'd come to love the Big Bend and its people, its lonely and majestic beauty. Why should we leave? Here on the Rio Grande we had found our home.

Twenty-eight

BUT TROUBLE WAS BREWING in the mountains south of the Rio Grande, the trouble out of which was to emerge the great revolutionist, Pancho Villa. This was trouble for which we were not responsible, and of which we knew almost nothing; but trouble, nevertheless, that would wreck our dreams of spending the rest of our lives on our homestead beside the river.

First, there were mere rumors of a small number of bandits raiding some of the more isolated mountain villages of northern Mexico. We paid little attention to them.

But in the months to come, the rumors persisted. According to grapevine reports, the bandits had increased in number and had begun to widen the scope of their operations. They called themselves the *Banderos Colorados,* or Red Flaggers, and it was said that their red flag emblem signified that they executed all captives.

There was fear in the eyes of our neighbors south of the river when they crossed to bring us these tales; and seeing this, I began to wonder. Yet, even then, busy as I was with teaching school and caring for my family and trying to improve my homestead, I failed to see what was really happening. I felt sympathy for my frightened neighbors; yet the trouble was still in Mexico, and I failed to see how it might concern me, a citizen of the United States, living north of the river.

Then in the fall of 1912, traveling with that unexplained swiftness of the border grapevine, came the news that the *Banderos Colorados* had struck at the river town of Ojinaga, where they not only ran off a herd of cattle and horses but shot down every man who opposed them.

This was getting close to home.

And then the bandits struck even closer. Only a few days later, Gormocindo Sanchez, one of my San Vicente pupils who was barely big enough to climb onto the sure-footed burro he rode, came jogging down the river trail to the spring. The bandits were approaching, he warned us.

This was really appalling news. There was no sort of organized force at San Vicente, Mexico, to repel the raiders. Gormocindo reported that the frightened villagers on the Mexican side were vacating the settlement, hurriedly transporting to the Texas side all their horses and cattle and whatever valuable possessions they could carry across the river.

But what was there to prevent the raiders from following them into Texas? Nothing, of course. Nothing, unless the fear of the United States army would stop them. What was to prevent them from coming on down to raid Boquillas and possibly killing us on the way? Again, nothing.

Some of the people were taking to the mountains, Gormocindo reported; and in sudden panic for the safety of Bessie and the children, I thought of following them.

But there was the matter of transportation. I still had the buckboard, but I had nothing to pull it with. And to strike out for the mountains afoot with a woman and two babies seemed to me to be inviting disaster.

Right there, I decided I could do worse than to stay where I was and hold what I had.

We thanked little Gormocindo for bringing us the news, filled his pockets with cookies, and watched him ride away. Then we turned to cleaning guns and gathering up all the ammunition in the house.

I went down to the river and broke the news to the bathers camped near the spring, suggesting that they all drive their wagons up to the house. The rock and adobe walls of the house ought to be bullet proof. Once inside, with guns to guard the windows and doors, we could stand off just about any sort of siege the bandits might attempt.

The bathers were eager to come spend the night with us; but the next morning, they were just as eager to get their wagons on the road toward Marathon.

Here was a chance to send Bessie and the children out to safety. But when I broached the subject, Bessie agreed to go only if I went.

"But if you stay, then we stay, too," she said firmly.

By then, I was determined to stay. We'd worked too hard to build our home here; I wasn't going to leave it to possible destruction by a bunch of bandits without putting up a fight.

So the campers left and Bessie and the children and I stayed. We spent the day getting ready to withstand a raid, should it come.

As an additional safeguard, I gathered up a supply of blankets and water and foodstuff and carried them to a nearby cave. Here, if necessary, I could hide my family for several days, giving the bandits time to move on.

By midafternoon, when no bandits had appeared, I saddled Boomer, hung my Winchester rifle on the saddle, buckled on a .45 six-shooter, and rode to San Vicente to find out what I could. There, I learned that the bandits were camped just across the river.

I rode back as quickly as possible to the home of my friend Cleofas, who promised to bring his rifle and help me guard my home as long as we might think necessary. Cleofas didn't seem concerned about leaving his family unprotected. He seemed to think if the bandits crossed the Rio Grande, it would be only to raid the homes and ranches of non-Mexicans.

Along with Tex, Cleofas and I kept vigil for several nights in a little *arroyo* about a hundred yards from the house. We were armed with a .30–30 rifle apiece; and for close-in fighting, I had on hand my six-shooter and shotgun.

And on the second night of our watch, the bandits did cross the river. It was late. There was almost no sound in the darkness except the wash of the river current and the occasional quavering cry of a Mexican screech owl, when Tex uttered a low growl. She bounced to her feet, with her bristles raised, and stood with her ears pointed toward the river crossing.

We heard them then, the splashing and stumbling of horses in the river and the creak of saddle leather. We fell on Tex, held her muzzle gripped tightly to keep her from barking. If the bandits came our way, we didn't want them aware of our presence. We wanted them close, and surprised when we opened up on them.

They came on across the river, some fifteen riders, judging by the sounds of their horses. We waited, tense and scared, but grimly determined to stand our ground. Time seemed to stand utterly still, and an eternity hung in those few moments.

Then, for some reason we never knew, the bandits halted at the mouth of Tornillo Creek, stalked around a little, then rode on back across the river.

And Cleofas and I breathed again.

We kept up our vigil for three more nights before we got word that the bandits had plundered both the Mexican villages of San Vicente and Boquillas, killed several men, then ridden back into their stronghold in the San Vicente Mountains.

Twenty-nine

THE FACT THAT THE BANDITS had decided not to raid across the Rio Grande into Texas on the night that Cleofas and I stood ready for them did not blind me to the possibility that the next time might be different.

I discussed this threat with several of my neighbors; and finally, Jesse Deemer and I made a trip to Marathon, where we petitioned the commander of Troop C, 14th Cavalry of the United States Army, to send troops to guard the border.

Twenty-five cavalrymen, under command of Lieutenant Collins, were sent down. They were stationed at La Noria, and men were sent in relays to ride the river from Boquillas to San Vicente.

Sight of Uncle Sam's soldiers guarding the river front renewed our confidence. For the time being, anyway, we felt safe from the bandits.

But within the next few days, we experienced a couple of domestic upsets in our own household that almost overshadowed the border trouble for us.

Bessie endured the first one alone. Soon after I left for school one morning, Tex started a savage baying outside, and Bessie went out to see what all the commotion was about.

Out near the corral, an old man with a club in his hand was frantically trying to beat off the fierce attacks of the raging Tex. He was shouting angrily at the dog and striking at her with the club. His shirt was wet through with sweat. His face was covered with a gray stubble. His gray hair stood wildly out all over his head. And when Bessie finally caught sight of his eyes, she nearly fainted. The lower lids were turned completely wrong-side out, forming a raw red half moon under each eye.

Bessie stood rooted to the ground, too frightened to know what to do. Finally, the man, catching sight of her, spoke in a perfectly normal voice, calmly and patiently.

"Lady," he said, "I wish you'd call this dog off. She looks like a real good watch dog, and I wouldn't want to have to hurt her."

Convinced at last that the man was harmless, Bessie called Tex off. The stranger was merely a customer who'd come to bathe, hoping to cure the ectropion that had ruined his lower eyelids.

Bessie invited him in. But Tex never was happy about the man, and continued to look on him as a threat to the family for as long as the visitor stayed.

Lovie was responsible for the second scare. She disappeared one day and we couldn't find her anywhere.

Just a little while before we missed her, I'd seen her and Lucille playing with a hive of bees that I'd captured in the hills. They were domestic Italian bees, so tame that not a one had stung when I robbed them. I'd fed them melted sugar a few times after I'd brought them in, and soon Lucille and Lovie were going out every day with a saucer of sugar and tapping on the box to call the bees out for another feed.

And now, here was Lucille, but no Lovie.

I thought first of the cliff, where Lucille had almost fallen to her death. The fence was there now to keep the children from falling off; but it was possible that Lovie had clambered over it.

A quick glimpse to the ground below relieved us of this terror.

We called. We searched the entire premises. We looked for tracks along the river bank, Tornillo Creek, all of the nearby hills and *arroyos*. But nowhere could we find a trace of her.

Bessie was almost frantic. I felt the same way. Every possibility in the world crossed my mind. I thought of the bandits and of what they would do to a helpless child, in their mood of wanton vengeance. I tried to reason that picture out of my mind, telling myself that the bandits were after supplies and horses and cattle, that there would be no point in their carrying off a child. But I still felt that clammy fear.

"You don't suppose—" Bessie said, and I could see she was fighting for control. "Well, you haven't seen any rattlers or their tracks around the house, have you?"

Of course, there was always that danger; but to calm Bessie, I told her it had been a long time since I'd seen a snake track anywhere around home.

We had searched for what seemed like hours, and found ourselves senselessly re-searching places we'd already combed over carefully. Finally, I told Bessie: "I'll go to San Vicente for help. Maybe if we get enough people out looking for her, we'll come across some sign."

I didn't tell Bessie, but I think she knew and felt the same way I was beginning to feel. I was about to give up hope. We walked back toward the house, a frantic and despairing couple.

Suddenly Tex left us and raced toward the corral. Not really expecting to find any sign, but unwilling to stop as long as there was any possibility left, I followed Tex.

She came back to meet me, wagging her tail and wearing a pleased expression on her intelligent face, and I felt the first hope I'd felt since we'd discovered that Lovie was gone.

Tex led me back to the corral and over to a haystack in the corner. She ran on around to the south side of the hay, and there lay Lovie, curled up in the warm sunshine, sound asleep, with her doll Susie clasped in her arms.

At that moment, I loved Tex nearly as much as I did any member of my family.

Thirty

LIEUTENANT COLLINS visited our cabin almost every day. Lovie and Lucille fell in love with him at once. That he usually had a pocketful of candy and would give them rides on his cavalry horse possibly had as much to do with that as the fact that he was a very personable young man, who might just as easily have gained the devotion of older girls—and probably did.

Every man on that patrol was likeable, for that matter, and their presence along the river was a continued source of comfort and pleasure to us. Rumors brought us news of more bandit raids along the river; but evidently the *Banderos Colorados* had learned of Uncle Sam's troops guarding the border here and didn't care to tangle with them. They stayed away all that winter.

It was during the time we had the river guards that the immigration officers began setting up a stricter border control. They issued an edict requiring everyone to cross the river at designated ports, during certain hours of the day. Mexican citizens caught on this side of the border illegally were taken to Alpine and on to El

Paso before they were deported through Juarez back into their own country. This forced some of them to walk as far as two hundred and fifty miles over rough country to get back to their own homes.

But Felix, the ten-year-old son of José Díaz, paid no attention to these new border restrictions. He'd always crossed the Rio Grande when and where he pleased; and when he learned of a goat-herding job on the Texas side, he crossed over, applied for the job, and got it.

A few days later he was picked up by the border patrol and was taken, with several other "outlaws," to Alpine on the regular deportation trip. There at Alpine, somebody with a little common sense sized the boy up and decided it would be working too great a hardship on him to send him all the way to Juarez. They withheld him from the train that went off that day, planning to take him back to his home territory as soon as any of the officers went back down that way.

Felix's captivity at Alpine lasted for several days. And a glorious captivity it was, too. This was the boy's first sight of a modern town, and the officers got a bang out of showing him around.

They found it pretty slow going, though. Felix stopped to shake hands with everyone he met on the streets. He lingered at all the shop windows. He stopped and stared at all the electric lights. And his greatest thrill came when the passenger train pulled up to the depot, whistling shrilly as it came, then stopping with a great hissing noise and big clouds of steam.

A few days later, the immigration officers deposited Felix at our place, and I watched while he thanked his captors for their courtesy, bade them and everyone there a hearty farewell, and waded the Rio Grande. He was running up the winding, rocky trail leading over a mountain when he passed out of our sight. And I have no doubt in the world that for days afterward he was still telling his family of all the wonderful sights and thrilling experiences of his perilous journey.

Thirty-one

THEN ONE DAY the grapevine brought us grave news all the way from Mexico City. President Madero had been murdered; a revolution was at hand.

On this same day, we received what for us was a more personal blow. Sergeant McEllaney, one of Lieutenant Collins' men, brought it. After swearing me to secrecy, McEllaney gave me Collins' message. Collins and all his men were being recalled to Marathon; from there they would be sent into foreign service. He advised me strongly to get my family away from the border at once.

That word shook me. I realized that Collins would not have risked court martial for revealing army secrets if he hadn't felt that our danger here was immediate and great.

I mulled it over for several hours. However temporary, the move would mean being away from the livelihood I had built up out of the springs. Then, too, I had just invested in a small stock of groceries in anticipation of starting a little store to supply my bathers.

I'd have to do something about that. And if we were gone very long from our source of income, it would mean beginning all over again in some other place and at some other way of making a living.

But the longer I thought, the more I came to know that there wasn't anything to do but leave and hope our absence would be short. Bessie and I discussed it for a little, but the danger to our children soon outweighed everything else.

That afternoon, I rode to San Vicente and hired Ysidro Sanchez to take Bessie and the children, with all our household goods, up to La Noria, where I felt they'd be safe with my friend Landrum until I could dispose of my stock of groceries.

We loaded Ysidro's wagon, with Bessie and me working in silence, avoiding each other's eyes. We soon had it done, and she and the little girls rode away.

A few days later, I joined them and we began our trip out of the Big Bend country. By now, Lovie was a big girl, nearly six years old, and Lucille was over three.

Once I saw Bessie look back in the direction of our abandoned homestead. Tears stood in her eyes. The country and its people had come to mean much to Bessie and me. I thought of the four brief years we'd spent there, of our struggle to make a home, and to make a livelihood. I thought of all it had given us—in the vast beauty of the river and its mountains, in my returned health, and, best of all, in the warm and loyal friendship of its people.

"Don't cry, Bessie," I comforted. "We'll be back. Just as soon as this trouble is over. We'll come back and take up right where we left off."

Thirty-two

BUT IT WAS A LONG TIME before we came back—fourteen years, in fact. And in that time, too many changes had taken place.

We had gone to El Paso to wait until the trouble on the Rio Grande was over. For a long time, we heard little from that part of the country; then we began to hear that after President Madero was killed, the bandits had increased. We learned that they occasionally made raids on the American side of the river, stealing cattle and robbing stores. At the end of three years, as late as 1916, there was still trouble. Glenn Springs was raided, buildings burned, and several people killed. We had to put our return to our homestead in the back of our minds.

I bought a couple of lots in El Paso and built a home, and we settled down. Bessie opened a flower shop; I built a filling station and hired a man to operate it while I worked as a carpenter. And it was there in El Paso that our sons Leroy and Joe were born and spent most of their childhood. Lovie and Lucille went to school; and when Lovie finished, she began teaching in one of the high schools.

Tragedy was to strike us there in El Paso. Lucille was killed the year before we returned to the homestead. She had been swimming in Washington Park and playing on the swings that hung out over the pool when she grasped one that had become charged by a faulty conduit. She was electrocuted instantly.

And so it was that we returned to our homestead without Lucille, and without Lovie. In their places were LeRoy, thirteen now, and Joe, who was eight.

And Bessie and I were no longer young. We and our entire family had changed.

But an even greater change had come over the land and the people along the Rio Grande since we'd left. During that time, the United States had been engaged in a great war. True, the war had been in Europe, but its effect had reached even down into such a faraway place as the Big Bend, starting a trend of land waste that still continues.

During the war, cattle prices and the prices of goats and sheep had soared. And to take advantage of these prices, ranchers had poured livestock into that vast region of grassland as fast as they could buy the animals. And now, where once I'd thought there was more grass than could ever be eaten off, I found no grass at all. Just the bare, rain-eroded ground. And where once beautiful pools of clear, cold water had stood in Tornillo Creek, now I found only great bars of sun-baked sand and gravel.

The same thing had happened to the fertile valley land where once my friend and neighbor Cleofas Natividad had grown such wonderful corn, beans, cushaws, and melons. Violent rain falling on the Tornillo Creek's watershed had encountered no grass to check its flow. So down the steep slopes it had come rolling, bringing the rocks and soil with it, carrying the debris down to dump it onto Cleofas' fertile acres, burying the good soil forever.

[153]

Abandoned dugouts, with the roofs fallen in, were all that was left of the dwellings that once had housed a happy and prosperous family. Cleofas was gone, as were most of the neighbors at San Vicente and Boquillas. All of them starved out by the blind greed and ignorance of men who had changed their paradise into a desert wasteland.

The few natives who had hung on were no longer the happy, self-sufficient people we'd known in the beginning. Their pride seemed broken, their natural enterprise and ingenuity gone. They'd learned enough of the ways of "civilization" to forsake the old arts and crafts that for centuries had fitted them for living in their own land. But they hadn't learned enough to fit them for living in the modern way. So now they existed in a sort of nebulous suspension between two cultures and were fitted for neither.

We came back in 1927. We built a store and established the Hot Springs postoffice. We built tourist courts for the convenience of customers, who, with the aid of automobiles and improved roads, came to the spring in ever-increasing numbers. We stayed there until 1942. And financially speaking, I suppose we could say that we prospered.

Yet, never again did we have that which we'd had in the beginning. Somehow, the brightness seemed gone from the land.

Index

CPSIA information can be obtained
at www.ICGtesting.com
Printed in the USA
LVHW051045260523
747967LV00004B/22